Abba's Lessons

30 stories of the lessons God teaches His children

Abba's Lessons

30 stories of the lessons God teaches His children

compiled and edited by

DEEDEE LAKE

ST JOSEPH, MISSOURI USA

Contents

Thy Will, Not Mine, Lord

Deb Gardner Allard

*"'For I know the plans I have for you,' declares the LORD,
'plans to prosper you and not to harm you, plans to
give you hope and a future.'" Jeremiah 29:11 NIV*

One thing I learned the hard way was that God's plans are the best ones.

I'd been enjoying my husband's duty station in Millington, Tennessee, because the people were super friendly, and we felt loved by the nearby church. But his assignment had been for advanced schooling, and he had graduated—time to move on. He came home that day waving a paper. "I've got to select three choices for my next duty station. They must be submitted today."

"Can I see the list?" Anxiety gripped me as Brian placed the paper in my shaking hands.

The list was plenty long, but I only read two entries—Japan and California. My mind blanked out after "California." The reason? Earthquakes. They petrified me. I'd read news reports about the quakes in California. When I came to my senses, I could only blubber. "I-I-I will never go to California. If you get orders there, I'll remain here until your next duty station."

Brian's face paled. "But you said we'd always stay together."

He was right. I'd made that promise. Holding hands with him, I bowed my head and asked God to send us anywhere but California because I refused to go there.

But Brian prayed, too, asking God to lead and guide us where He wanted to send us, and for Him to go before us, protect us, calm our fears, and use us to further His Word.

Ooh, I was upset by his prayer. "What if God sends us to California?"

"If He does, He'll take care of us. You have to trust Him, Deb. You prayed the other day for more faith. Well, have faith that God has far more wisdom than we do. He'll send us where we should go."

Somehow, right then and there, I knew where we were headed.

Two weeks later, as I was packing supplies for our road trip to California—yes, California—tears ran down my face. "Are you the One sending us, God? How will I know this is from you and not a random selection courtesy of the Navy?"

God answered my prayers in many ways. A fellow graduate from Brian's class was also given orders to California. He and his wife and two children headed there a week before us. Bob called Brian from California with a warning. "Send Deb and the kids to live with family. It's too expensive out here. We have to pay three times our rent in Tennessee. Plus, the landlord asked for the first and last months' rents and a steep security deposit in advance. And the place won't become available for a month. We're spending every last cent to live in the Navy Lodge until then. We'll be eating soup from cans in California."

Panic gripped me. Maybe it wasn't God sending us there.

Brian thanked Bob for the information. "I'm sorry about what you're going through, Bob, but we're asking God for help.

If you knew Jesus, you could ask Him for help too. We'll be praying for you." After hanging up, Brian shared Bob's story with me.

I fiddled with the packing paper in my hands. "Maybe the kids and I should live with my mother." But if we did, I'd be parted from the love of my life.

"No way." Brian wrapped his arms around me. "Remember about faith and trust? We'll ask God to find us a place. And we'll trust Him since He chose our new duty station."

Such profound wisdom from my hubby. He taught me, a Catholic gal, so much about trusting God. I developed a personal relationship with Jesus because of my husband. That day, Brian called our church's prayer chain and asked them to pray for affordable and available housing for our little family at our next duty station.

Our trip to California in our old maroon sedan had its challenges, but on the third day, we pulled up to the Navy Lodge. After Brian checked us in, we placed our suitcases in the room, and the children began to cry, "We're thirsty!" What happened next was the first miracle but not the last one God ever did for us.

"I'll get some sodas. Then we can decide where to go for dinner." Brian left for the canteen while we explored the room.

Fifteen minutes later, he returned, waving an index card. "Look what I found on their bulletin board!"

It was a handwritten advertisement: House for Rent. Will negotiate occupancy. The date posted was that very day.

Excited, I hollered, "Call right away!"

After one ring, a man answered Brian's phone call. He said the rental was still available, and he'd meet us at the address in an hour. We were a little fearful about coming up with the first and last months' rents as well as a security deposit. How would we have money for groceries? We prayed and asked God to please handle everything for us.

With forty-five minutes left before the meeting, we quickly bought fast food in town, then, bellies satisfied, we headed to the rental house. It was nestled on a cul-de-sac in a quiet residential neighborhood. The home's teal stucco exterior displayed gorgeous rose bushes on both sides of its entry steps. And the grassy front yard beckoned our children to tumble and play while we waited. I was beyond excited to see the inside.

The owner arrived soon after we did and gave us a tour. The place had more footage than we imagined. But the inside needed the carpets cleaned, walls painted, and debris and trash removed. "If you wouldn't mind handling these things— I'll waive the usual fees, make the first month's rent free, and bring the paint," the owner said.

"That sounds fair." Brian accepted the keys while I tried to control my excitement.

"I hope you enjoy living here." The man beamed as he headed out the door.

The first thing we did was hold hands and thank the Lord for working everything together for us even better than we'd hoped. He made what was impossible—possible. We hadn't been in California for more than a few hours, and already we had keys to a home without a penny from our pockets. With God, all things are possible.

Over the three years, we learned why God brought us to California. Bob sent Brian a card. He said because of what God did for us, he and his family accepted the Lord. We were ecstatic for them.

And as for Brian and me, within a couple weeks, God led us to an amazing little church that did in-depth expository Bible teaching on Sunday mornings, evenings, and Wednesday evenings—it reminded us of a Bible college.

During our time in California, we learned deep Bible teaching based on the Hebrew and Greek texts. We learned God is in control. We can't tell Him what to do, we can only ask. But His plans are to help us and not to harm us. I learned to seek His will and not mine.

If I had it to do over again, I'd leap at the opportunity. God's plans, indeed, were to bless us abundantly. And while we lived in California, we never experienced more than a mild earth tremor, no major earthquakes. God's will—His plans—are the best ones.

Prayer

Dear Lord, you're a mighty God who can supply our needs if we ask and wait for answers with complete faith. Sometimes your answers take hours, days, months, or years, but you always answer. Help us to understand that when you say no or lead us in a different direction, you have a specific reason—to give us hope and a future. Thank you, Lord, for your infinite wisdom and never-ending love. In Jesus' name. Amen.

The Love of the Father is Restful

Betts Baker

"Come to Me, all you who labor and are heavy laden, and I will give you rest. Take My yoke upon you and learn from Me, for I am gentle and lowly in heart, and you will find rest for your souls. For My yoke is easy and My burden is light." Matthew 11:28–30 NKJV

Not long after the birth of our third child, I got sick with what we thought was the flu. I couldn't seem to recover. Eventually, my husband took me to the doctor, who diagnosed hepatitis A. Although I was very sick, we weren't too worried. Everyone said a month of rest would do it.

But somehow, that wasn't the case. Because people feared contracting the illness, it was difficult to get help. My fatigue persisted. After four months, my husband moved the children and me to my mother's house and left us in her care.

My mother installed me in a room at the far end of the house. There, for the first time in a very long time, I had nothing to do except lie in bed. I slept for hours. When I woke, I gazed out the windows at my mother's large garden. Light and shadow dappled the trees as the sun moved across the sky. I watched leaves emerge and flowers bud and bloom as spring ripened into summer. In the quiet of those days, God seemed very near. By my mother's hand, He had rescued my husband and me from the brink of collapse and provided this great rest. I felt bathed by His love.

As I gained strength, I read short passages of the Bible each day. Afterward, I lay contemplating God's ways. I had never heard of anyone with hepatitis A getting well so slowly. God could have healed this illness quickly or even prevented it. Instead, He allowed it, removing me completely from my active life abroad. I'd been obeying Him there, learning the language, and making friends with our neighbors. This illness forced me to abandon the friendships I had worked so hard to develop. If I was obeying, why had He allowed it? Yet God didn't seem angry with me. His love seemed unaffected by my inactivity. His blessings and His love poured over me every day, filling me with an unexpected peace.

Month by month, I became more certain God was pleased with me just as I was. I had misunderstood Him. He wasn't focused on goals after all. He valued *me*, not what I accomplished. Wonder and joy grew in me.

One day I read Matthew 11:28–30. The last line caught my attention: "For my yoke is easy and my burden is light." In my experience, they had been heavy. Jesus himself had said the path was narrow and the way hard, so I had shouldered the work. Yet here, Jesus said, "Take My yoke upon you, and learn from Me...*and you will find rest*" (author's emphasis). My heart hungered for this kind of rest. I wanted to know more.

Over the following weeks, I examined my pre-illness life.

Although I had prayed about God's will, I hadn't really allowed Him to order my days. I had added to whatever He made clear, hurrying from one duty to the next. I had created heavy loads for myself and carried them alone. No wonder I had become tired.

Now I could see that all the striving—the lists of phone calls and visits, the urgency to study the language—had been of my own making, not His. Of course, He wanted me to obey, but only what He asked of me and yoked with Him, learning by His side, not alone.

The illness had given me time to recognize God's love. He had removed my busywork so I would turn my face to Him just as the flowers outside my window turned their faces to the sun. The rest I enjoyed during this long recovery could continue to be part of my life with God. If I listened to Him and walked with Him, He would give me peace instead of a treadmill of duties. My heart sighed a deep yes.

Do you secretly believe God is a hard taskmaster, requiring a life of strenuous duty and obligation?

Stop and reconsider. Instead of scurrying to do things for Him, take time to sit by His side, gaze into His face, and listen to His voice. The truth is that God wants you to spend time with Him. Accept His loving care and peaceful pace. Let Him lead and guide. Do what He shows you without adding anything. Then you will have joy.

Prayer

Dearest Father, I confess I have wronged You by believing You are harsh and demanding. I have filled my days with activity, believing this would please You, but I have not truly listened to You. Forgive me. Help me better understand and accept Your loving kindness. Enable me to give up laboring for Your love and approval. Teach me how to be still and to love You in return. In Jesus' name, amen.

I Will Sing There

Laura L. Bradford

*"Therefore, behold, I will allure her, and bring her into
the wilderness, and speak comfortably unto her. And I
will give her vineyards from thence, and the valley of
Achor for a door of hope: and she shall sing there, as in
the days of her youth, and as in the day when she came
up out of the land of Egypt." Hosea 2:14–15 KJV*

Excited to learn new praise songs, I started playing Emily's
album as soon as I got home from church. Emily had
given each family a copy of an album she'd created to
teach us her favorite Scripture songs based on the King James
Version of the Bible.

Her album began with two songs I already knew, so I had
fun singing along. Then a new song began that had such a
sweet melody. I listened in awe as Emily sang, "He has wooed
me into the wilderness to the valley of Achor to betroth me in
faithfulness."

That opening line intrigued me since our family had just
moved into our dream home on twenty acres of forested
mountainside only half a mile from wilderness. Emily's song

17

made me wonder if it was the Lord who had "wooed" us into this delightful wilderness to draw us closer to His heart.

Grabbing a list Emily had given us with Scripture references to her songs, I saw that the soothing refrain was taken from Hosea 2:14–15, "Therefore, behold, I will allure her, and bring her into the wilderness, and speak comfortably unto her. And I will give her vineyards from thence, and the valley of Achor for a door of hope: and she shall sing there, as in the days of her youth, and as in the day when she came up out of the land of Egypt."

Yes! That valley sounds as beautiful as our place!

God had blessed our wilderness home with so many delightful things: nearby mountain peaks, abundant wildlife, towering pines, a roaring creek, and so much more. Since Hosea 2 mentions that the woman sang like she had in her youth, I assumed the valley of Achor must have been a lovely place, much like our property. Then I glanced at a definition in the footnotes of my Bible. Much to my surprise, it stated the Hebrew word Achor meant trouble.

What? Why would this woman be motivated to sing in a place of trouble?

More research revealed the woman in this story was an illustration of Israel. Hosea had been given this prophetic word while the Assyrian empire held Israel captive. The wilderness Hosea mentioned was one of…suffering! Israel had come under enemy rule because her people had turned from God to worship useless idols. Israel's captivity was God's way of awakening the nation to her corruption. However, Hosea's prophetic story let Israel know her captivity wouldn't be permanent. It was meant to turn God's beloved people back to Him.

Wow. That sounds like my life story…and my husband's.

Early in life, my husband, John, and I had felt God tugging at our hearts. But in our teen years, we'd pushed Him aside to follow fleshly whims. During that time of rebellion, John and I met and married. Yet, God wasn't willing to let our rebellion continue. A few years into our marriage, my husband was diagnosed with the incurable nerve disease multiple sclerosis. By then, MS was already robbing John of the ability to walk without support from crutches. My husband's disability put an abrupt end to the self-serving life we'd been striving to build.

Overwhelmed in our valley of trouble, I'd surrendered to Jesus and become a new creation. When John saw God's power changing me, he started accompanying me to church. However, my husband didn't immediately become a new creation. Instead of clinging to Jesus, John leaned on his powerful intellect and twisted sense of humor to cope with the devastating paralysis of MS.

When I'd heard him spouting dirty jokes in front of our young son, it made me angry. Nevertheless, as I looked to God for help, interesting things began happening in my heart. I learned to love and respect my husband despite sinful tendencies. I also experienced unexplainable joy in God's presence. And I developed a passion for singing God's praises.

Studying Hosea made me realize our lovely mountainside wilderness could never have turned my heart to God. Instead, the devastation of John's MS had served as our valley of Achor. In that wilderness of trouble, God "betrothed me in faithfulness" just as He'd done for wayward Israel.

While I marveled at the mercy God had shown to me, I received fresh hope that He'd yet do the same for John.

Thankful for the revelation that God sent our wilderness experience with MS to change our lives, I restarted Emily's album. I lifted my hands to heaven when her sweet voice crooned, "And I will sing there. I will sing there as in the days of my youth. In the valley of Achor, I will sing. For there, my

God has provided a door of hope. And it's there I will stand and sing."

"Yes!" I said with determination, rising to my feet. "I will sing in this valley of Achor. I will sing to you, God, and never give up."

That passage from Hosea became my theme song for the next fifteen years. While paralysis gradually enveloped John's body, I refused to stop singing praises to God. Finally, when John had no power left to fight against God, he surrendered his will to Jesus. My husband's wilderness journey ended a short time later as God opened His "door of hope" and welcomed John home.

Despite my widowhood, I've refused to spend my days in grief. For I've realized that it's not the beauty of life that drew me to God, but the troubles. Awed by the mercy He continues to show me, I will sing praises in this valley of Achor until God calls me home.

Prayer

Abba, I pray I'm able to look past losses to focus on what is gained by going through trials. I know You are with me and will never leave me. Thank you for loving me so much more than I know. In Jesus' name, amen.

Hearing vs. Doing God's Word

Catherine Ulrich Brakefield

"But be doers of the word, and not hearers only, deceiving yourselves. For if anyone is a hearer of the word and not a doer, he is like a man observing his natural face in a mirror; for he observes himself, goes away, and immediately forgets what kind of man he was. But he who looks into the perfect law of liberty and continues in it, and is not a forgetful hearer but a doer of the work, this one will be blessed in what he does." James 1:22–25 NKJV

Glassy-eyed, like a deer caught in headlights, Juan* looked at me and then to my husband and said in broken English, "My girlfriend is pregnant. She's afraid when her parents find out that her mother will force her to have an abortion." Juan knew he'd done a sinful act.

He was an illegal alien who came over the border from Mexico. He worked full-time at an equestrian facility and worked for us part-time. We'd sort of taken Juan under our wings, inviting him to Wednesday church services where there was a Spanish interpreter who could translate the preacher's sermon to him. On Sundays, he'd attend a Catholic church in Imlay City.

His girlfriend, Jane*, had just turned eighteen; she would graduate that June from high school. Jane spoke to me about marrying Juan. Her parents were against the marriage because Juan wasn't a citizen, and she was too young. I agreed with her parents.

In Michigan, back in 2015, though there was no law exempting illegals from deportation, if an illegal married a citizen and had a baby, the authorities left him alone.

"Juan, I warned you about getting, well, too close with her," Edward, my husband, said. "Do you love her?"

Juan hesitated. "Yes, I love her and will take good care of her and the baby."

My feelings said to stay out of this. No way did I want to be part of this deception in hiding Jane's pregnancy from her parents. Pray! Right. God, I'm doing my Christian duty and praying! I felt the pull of the Holy Spirit. Knowing what you should do and doing it are two different things. I felt as convicted as Juan and very close to becoming a hearer of the Word and not doing what I felt God's Holy Spirit whispered in my heart.

A soul lived in the womb of this young girl. Pray, yes, but God urged me to do more. Lord, I argued, I'm praying. Can't that suffice? After all, I am doing something—I'm praying. But I felt the Holy Spirit wanted me to do more.

The Holy Spirit revealed God's truth. Abortion was not in my vocabulary—or God's. She can find help at the Crisis Pregnancy Center. Lord, can I walk away from this debacle then?

Juan and Jane met Edward and me at Taco Bell. I handed her the information from the Center, including the name to contact for an appointment and a doctor who would take care of her needs. I asked her if I went with her to tell her mother about the pregnancy, would her mother demand an abortion?

Fear lit like a glaring caution light across Jane's face. "Yes. But when I have the baby, I know my mother will fall in love with him or her. Juan will be a loving father and husband."

"To make any relationship work, you need a threefold cord. Do you know God and His Son, Jesus Christ?" I asked.

"No, not really."

I pulled out a pocket Bible and flipped to John 3:16, then 1 Corinthians 13. I told her Jesus knew her even if she didn't know Him and that He died for her. Then I gave her my pocket Bible and asked her to read through the Gospel According to John every chance she got. I told them that in God's eyes, they were married, and I told Juan he needed to buy a ring for Jane. She thought they needed to put the money elsewhere. But the Crisis Pregnancy Center endorsed what I had said about purchasing a ring. Jane wore it every time she went to her doctor's appointments.

When she started wearing baggy tops, her mom and dad told her to watch her weight and repeatedly grumbled, "You'd better not be pregnant."

Since both Juan and Jane wanted to get married, Juan made the arrangements at the courthouse. We were the witnesses. I was getting dragged in deeper and deeper. I had not told Jane's parents about her pregnancy, and now here I was performing the role her mother should be doing. Waiting for our turn, Jane's hopes and dreams of a bright future tumbled out like liquid sunshine. "Someday, I want a wedding where I come down the aisle in a beautiful white flowing dress."

A sickening feeling swept over me. I'm a mother. I would be devasted if someone took my place like I was doing in the case of Jane's mother. God, when the baby arrives, have Jane's parents welcome Juan and the baby into their family.

God says nothing is impossible. Put your faith in Him, read His Bible, and follow and obey what He says to do. "Dear Jesus, please bless this baby and this covenant created in haste. In Jesus' name, we pray."

I gave them Bibles with their names engraved in silver on the burgundy covers as wedding presents. Within the pages of Scriptures to guide them, I placed several $20 bills.

The time for the baby's delivery arrived. Jane called her mom, telling her she was about to give birth to their first grandchild. I got balloons and presents ready.

With tears in her eyes, Jane said her mother refused to come to the hospital, but her aunt hadn't. Juan was a doting dad.

I readied my small studio apartment for the family, praying God would work His love on Jane's parents. When Juan and Jane didn't arrive at the apartment as expected, I called Juan.

Jane's mom had relented! Her parents allowed the couple to live with them in their home, and her mother helped take care of her new granddaughter.

A few months later, I was invited to the home. The adorable baby was dressed in a bright pink dress and wrapped in a powder pink blanket. Her doting grandmother gave the infant and me a huge smile.

Their little granddaughter, a beautiful dark-haired and bright-eyed child is the shining light within her grandmother's and grandfather's eyes. Only our loving Lord and Savior could work this miracle of love!

I said yes to God and then wanted out. I learned a valuable lesson. Hearing vs. doing—knowing what you should do and doing it takes obedience and determination. When we do what God has instructed us to do, He changes lives in amazing ways!

Prayer

Lord, please give me the courage and wisdom to act when I hear your voice telling me to move, to go, to speak, or to give. I know you love me and the ones I cross paths with. Help me to be slow to speak and quick to listen to your voice. In Jesus' name, amen.

*Names changed to protect privacy.

The Mighty Power of Praise

Debra L. Butterfield

*"Around midnight Paul and Silas were praying
and singing hymns to God." Acts 16:25a NLT*

Paul and Silas had been severely beaten and imprisoned, yet here they were, at midnight, praying and singing hymns. They could have complained about their circumstances or even groaned in pain, yet they chose to pray and praise God instead.

The Bible is filled with praise; the book of Psalms in particular. But many people think praise is a feel-good thing done only in church. I've learned it's so much more than that.

Several years ago, I contracted shingles. It started with a pain just under my right shoulder blade. I thought it was my gallbladder (from a previous similar experience) or muscle issues from a work desk that wasn't ergonomic-friendly. But the morning I noticed a rash on my chest, I knew immediately what was wrong. My mother had suffered from shingles a few years prior to me with the same onset of symptoms and in the exact same place on her body.

Because I don't particularly like going to the doctor, and I knew what was wrong, I self-medicated. My pain level during the day was minimal and Tylenol managed it. I went about my usual work. Nighttime was an altogether different story.

The pain grew intense around 2:00 each night and didn't let up until dawn. I gutted it out for several days (because that's what Marines do, even those of us who are no longer in active service). I used two types of pain killers and found a prone position on the couch that actually brought some relief.

In addition, I added liberal doses of prayer. I prayed for the Lord to take away the pain, and I claimed my healing according to 1 Peter 2:24c NLT, "By his wounds you are healed."

After several nights like this, I was worn down and the pain became excruciating. As I struggled to find the position that would bring some relief, the Lord brought Paul and Silas to mind.

"A mob quickly formed against Paul and Silas, and the city officials ordered them stripped and beaten with wooden rods. They were severely beaten, and then they were thrown into prison. The jailer was ordered to make sure they didn't escape. So the jailer put them into the inner dungeon and clamped their feet in the stocks. …Suddenly, there was a massive earthquake, and the prison was shaken to its foundations. All the doors immediately flew open, and the chains of every prisoner fell off!" (Acts 16:22–24, 26 NLT).

Undoubtedly, their pain level and circumstances were more dire than mine. Yet they chose to praise God and it brought deliverance. If they could praise God in the middle of all that, so could I. I worked my way off the couch, and then I began praising God in word and song.

I must have spent an hour or more in praise and worship. The pain subsided and I was able to lie down and sleep. Yes, it drove me to the doctor the next day, but I had learned a valuable lesson: praise is a spiritual weapon.

Merriam-Webster's Online Dictionary defines *praise* as "to express a favorable judgment of: commend; to glorify (a god or saint) especially by the attribution of perfections."

When I praise God, my focus is on Him, not on my problem. I am ushered into His presence, and there I am much more open to receive from Him. Praise is a doorway to God.

He has taught me that when I'm fighting a tough battle, praising Him gives me the focus I need and the strength to battle on. He gave me another great example of the power of praise in King Jehoshaphat.

A great multitude had arrayed itself against the king. On learning this, the king immediately sought the Lord.

The Lord answered, "Take your positions; then stand still and watch the LORD's victory. He is with you, O people of Judah and Jerusalem. Do not be afraid or discouraged. Go out against them tomorrow, for the LORD is with you!" (2 Chronicles 20:17b NLT).

The following day "the king appointed singers to walk ahead of the army, singing to the LORD and *praising* him for his holy splendor" (2 Chronicles 20:21b NLT, emphasis added). They won the battle.

They left Jerusalem praising the Lord and they returned in the same manner.

The power of praise can be applied in every trial I face. It is not only a time for me to express my love to Him, but it is also a mighty weapon of warfare.

Prayer

ather, I want to spend time today praising You. I will sing your praises using Scripture and simply telling You how much I love You. That brings joy and peace to me. Thank you for giving me the gift and spiritual battle tool of praise. You are a good God. In Jesus' name, amen.

Stuck in a Rut

Sandra Kay Chambers

"Trust in the LORD with all your heart and lean not on your own understanding; in all your ways submit to him, and he will make your paths straight." Proverbs 3:5–6 NIV

I sped through the bleak countryside on my way to the retreat center. Spring was on the way, but the weather was gloomy, like my state of mind. I was happy to have been invited to the annual women's retreat and looked forward to seeing old friends from my former church.

Former. That sounded so final. So definite. Even though it had been ten months since we moved, I felt like I still belonged there. I had started a prayer ministry and had given my heart and soul to fulfill it. Now, there was a deep void and a sense of uselessness in my life. Had God really wanted us to move? If so, why did it still hurt so much? But this weekend, I would hide the pain and pretend things were fine.

When I arrived at the retreat center, I was given a packet that contained a conference brochure with the schedule for the weekend. I scanned the page and noticed the topic of one speaker: "When You've Had It, and You Want to Give Up…

Don't!" Easy enough for the speaker to say, I mumbled to myself.

Friday evening was light and fun with several activities and fellowship. It felt great to be among old friends again. Saturday would be a full day with main speakers and small group breakouts. I sat through the Saturday morning session with a growing restlessness. As I squirmed in my seat, I heard the speaker say, "It's okay to ask God why?"

But I've been asking why, I complained to God silently, and I still don't have an answer!

As soon as the session ended, I dashed to my car. I had to take a break. The conference stirred up all the frustration and anger I felt toward God for disrupting my life. I decided I wouldn't return for the small group breakout session. I didn't feel like talking and sharing intimately with others. Instead, I would drive through the countryside and take some scenic shots with the new camera I'd brought along.

As I rounded a curve in the road, I saw a farmhouse with an old-fashion clothesline and clothes flapping in the breeze. Thinking it would make a quaint photo, I quickly swerved the car onto a grassy area off the road. When I stepped out of the car, I sank into the wet, muddy ground. Spotting the small stream just a few yards from my car, I knew I was in trouble.

Back inside the car, I tried to pull forward. My tires spun hopelessly. I put the car in reverse and tried to back up, but the more I tried to free the car, the deeper my tires dug into the ruts. Finally, I turned off the car and sat there wondering what to do. My only choice seemed to be to walk to the farmhouse and ask to use their phone to call a tow truck.

"I seem to be stuck in the mud," I explained to the tall stocky man who answered the door. Behind him, I could see another man lacing up his boots.

"Maybe we can help get you out," he said, pulling on his jacket. A third man followed, and soon all three were attempting to push my car free. After several failed attempts, one of the men came to the car window and asked if the brake was off. In my panic, I had forgotten to release the emergency brake. Feeling rather stupid, I released the brake and put the car in drive. With the next push, the vehicle surged forward. I was free and back on the road. I offered to pay them, but they refused and waved me off.

As I looked back in the rearview mirror, I saw all three men wiping off the mud flung on them as they dislodged my car. Tears welled in my eyes as I thought about the last several months and the mud of my complaints and doubts that I had flung at God while spinning my spiritual tires. I was stuck in a spiritual rut and was trying to figure it out on my own instead of giving it to God and trusting Him. Meanwhile, He was patiently waiting for me to take off the brake and trust Him to get me out of the rut and back on His path. As tears streamed down my face, I confessed my sin of doubt and unbelief and asked God to forgive me and help me trust Him with my future.

Life is full of changes that often bring frustration, doubt, and fear into our lives. We can't understand the why, and it's easy to get stuck in a spiritual rut, but God can't rescue us when we put on the brake and resist Him. As today's Scripture tells us, we need to stop looking to our own understanding and submit to and trust God with all our hearts. He loves us, wants the best for us, and has promised to lead and guide us and make our paths straight.

Prayer

Lord, help us know You are always there, ready to help us get out of our ruts and back on Your path if we just take off the brake and trust You. I know we all face difficult changes in our lives, and we can get stuck in a spiritual rut trying to figure things out on our own when all we need to do is submit to You, God, and trust You to get us out and make our paths straight. In Jesus' name, amen.

Choices and Change

Tamara Clymer

"He will not crush the weakest reed or put out a flickering candle. He will bring justice to all who have been wronged." Isaiah 42:3 NLT

uzz. Buzz. Buzz… My cell phone broke the silence with a nearly steady rhythm of annoying alerts. Some messages extended warm wishes. The rest were full of concern. I ignored them all.

I sat alone in the deserted waiting room in a Denver hospital late at night on my fiftieth birthday in the middle of the Covid pandemic. I was lucky they allowed me in the hospital at all, but I wasn't feeling blessed that evening. I wasn't feeling much of anything.

My mind was a numb, jumbled mess. In the last twenty-four hours I learned my husband didn't have a migraine headache or a sinus infection. Shad had a mass inside his brain—about the size of one of those Cutie oranges our kids love so much.

Now I was waiting to find out what the surgeons had found. I was hoping for a pocket of fluid or something benign they could just remove, but an uneasy feeling rolled around in the pit of my stomach.

35

I looked up at the sound of footsteps as the neurosurgeon stepped into the waiting room. His eyes drifted over the empty seats until he spotted me at a corner table in the back. He still wore a surgical mask, like we all did in those days, and while I couldn't see his face, I could see the grim look in his eyes as he made his way toward me.

This wasn't going to be good.

He plopped into the chair across from me and with what I could tell was all the courage he could muster, the words began tumbling out of his mouth.

"Seven centimeters…Got most of it…Testing…"

He stopped for a second. I could sense he didn't want to say the next part. His eyes shifted to the tabletop between us before moving back up to my face. He took a deep breath and forever changed my life.

"It is glioblastoma."

Boom. Those three words sucked the air out of the room.

Cancer. I am a veterinarian's wife. I know words ending in -oma usually mean cancer.

He waited a second, then stood. Placing a hand gently on my shoulder, he gave it a light pat. "I'm sorry," he said. Then he turned and walked away.

I immediately grabbed my cell phone off the seat next to me. Asking Dr. Google for a second opinion is rarely a good idea.

"Malignant brain tumor…very aggressive…grows fast… spreads quickly…there is no cure."[1]

I fell back in my chair.

My father *and* my husband are dying.

Honestly, we're all dying. It's just a matter of time, but for

---

1. https://www.webmd.com/cancer/brain-cancer/what-is-glioblastoma

these amazing men of God, that time was now measured in days, weeks…if we were lucky, maybe months.

My dad was diagnosed with liver cancer about a year before Shad's trip to the ER. At the time we thought Dad's cancer would be manageable. The doctors would operate, it would be contained, and after some chemo and radiation he would get better.

But they couldn't do surgery and before we knew it the cancer had taken over his entire body.

And did I tell you my mother has Alzheimer's?

I have to admit, I struggled a lot with my faith at that point. I didn't question the validity of it. I wondered if it was strong enough to help me survive the enemy's barrage.

Unfortunately, faith doesn't grow in a vacuum. Nothing does. I wish it did. Life would be so much easier, but then again…we would be little more than robots if it did. After all, how strong would our faith be if we didn't exercise it?

It definitely wouldn't be strong enough to get us through this stuff.

For faith to grow, it has to be used, stretched, tried, exercised, worked, and tested. Only then can it be strengthened.

When I was in high school, I was a decent little athlete. Okay, not really, but I tried. I played basketball, volleyball, baseball (yes, on the boys' team. We didn't have softball.) I even tried my hand at track.

But I hated practice.

Oh, goodness how I hated practice. Especially basketball practice. I despised it. Running up and down the court for no other reason other than to get in shape. Ugh. I despise running to this day. But I did it because I loved to play the game.

Our coach was relentless. Day after agonizing day, our coach put us through grueling sprint drills. And we were timed. If we didn't do the whole thing in thirty-two seconds, we had to run the sprint again...often to the point of losing our lunch. Then we only had about thirty seconds before we had to get back up to the line to do it all over again.

I'm tired just thinking about it.

But you know what? After the second day, we didn't miss our times anymore.

A week later we had legs and lungs of steel.

By our first game, running up and down the court for an hour wasn't such an ordeal. All because we ran those stupid sprints.

I'm not sure where Coach Ellis picked up his conditioning regimen, but I sometimes wonder if they were God-inspired. Consider this...

"The temptations in your life are no different from what others experience. And God is faithful. He will not allow the temptation to be more than you can stand. When you are tempted, he will show you a way out so that you can endure" (1 Corinthians 10:13 NLT).

When Paul used the word *temptation*, he was using the Greek word *peirasmos* meaning "a putting to proof" (*Strong's Concordance*).

So what does proof mean? *Merriam-Webster's Dictionary* says it is "a test applied to articles or substances to determine whether they are of standard or satisfactory quality. (www. merriam-webster.com/dictionary/proof).

That test is experience.

So, by exercising, our muscles and lungs were strengthened. And by our experience our faith is proven.

And those experiences aren't any different from what anyone else faces.

We all have trials...financial troubles, illness, heartache.

Our kids act up. Our cars break down. Cats chew laptop cords…dogs pee on our white capris.

Everyone has the same stuff…big and small. But not everyone leans on God. That is where the difference comes in.

His help is available 24/7, which means…

"Either our trials will be proportioned to our strength, or strength will be supplied in proportion to our temptations" (*Matthew Henry's Commentary,* pg 2262).

I like that.

Either God won't let the tough stuff be more than I can handle, or He will give me the strength to get through it.

I'm finding that out firsthand right now, but you know what? God is faithful.

I will not be naive enough to say all this is not more than I can handle…It is, but I can confidently say that when Dad went Home, God held me up, and He continues to hold me up through Shad's treatments and every visit with my mom that shows decline. He has supplied strength (beyond my understanding) so I can put one foot in front of the other through this trial and see His hand all along the way.

And He will do the same for you.

"There is no valley so dark but he can find a way through it, no affliction so grievous but he can prevent, or remove, or enable us to support it, and in the end overrule it to our advantage (*Matthew Henry's Commentary* pg 2262).

God may allow our trials to exhaust us. He may let it get overwhelming. But He won't let it break us…only we can allow that.

The good news is we all have a choice. We can let our trials break us, or we can choose to cling to the One who made us and trust Him.

Trusting Him allows our faith to grow. It isn't fun. It isn't pretty, it is often messy and painful, and it certainly isn't what any of us would choose.

But it can be life changing.

The kind of change that you look back on and realize the pain was worth it, because you wouldn't be where you are right now if you hadn't faced it head on.

We have a choice, my friend. We can either buckle under the trial or we can choose to grow our faith by holding the hand of the One who loves us even more than our daddies do.

I hope you'll choose to grow.

Prayer

Father, hold me up. In the midst of this trial, please be my everything. Allow me to see things from your eternal perspective. Guide me so my faith will grow and please let me feel the love I know You have for me. Be my everything, God, I pray. In Jesus name, amen.

Finding the Will to Keep Working

Sally Cressman

"[F]or the people had a mind to work." Nehemiah 4:6b ESV

When we seek God's help, He will give us the will to do our seemingly small tasks and His sometimes impossible and toilsome assignments.

I learned to swim at the age of fifty-five.

It wasn't that I didn't know how to—I'd just never done it. I'd paid hundreds of dollars to listen in and watch my youngest take swim lessons and train with a club team. I'd even trained as a "stroke-and-turn" judge so I could identify a legal stroke. I've endured many sauna-like venues, sharing the same humid space with hundreds of others while I languished away on scorching metal bleachers, willing an official to announce an adult-only swim session.

Yet, I'd never thought of taking swimming lessons for myself until the summer of 2015. I sat in a climate-controlled venue and watched my daughter swim back and forth for seventeen minutes in the one-mile event.

41

I can do that. I should do that. Maybe I should even get in the water once.

Not swim a mile, mind you, but get in the pool and try all those strokes and drills I'd witnessed over the past ten years.

The next day I bought goggles, a cap, a kickboard, and a swimsuit and biked down to the neighborhood pool. I jumped in. It was only three feet deep, but water splashed my face. I spent that summer flailing and failing, arriving early in the mornings when the pool opened and neighbors had not yet finished their first cup of coffee.

Why does it look so easy when my daughter swims? Why do my goggles keep filling up? How do you turn your head to breathe without gulping water?

I humbled myself and asked for help with the equipment and the actual swimming. My daughter shot a video of me and gave me exercises to start. I worked on those drills day after day. One lap exhausted me. I gasped and waited a few minutes before I tried another one. Zig-zagging all over, I bonked my head on the pool's edge numerous times.

When the outdoor pool closed for the summer, my only choice was to swim in a nearby Olympic-sized indoor pool where seasoned athletes swim. I mustered the courage to go. As I stood on the edge, the shimmering body of water intimidated me.

I don't deserve to be here. I should go home and give this nonsense up. I'll never make it across to the other side. Lord, don't let me be humiliated and require the lifeguard. Get me across this pool and back.

Hesitating to take the plunge, I dipped my toes, splashed my body, adjusted my goggles, dipped my toes, and adjusted my goggles. A guy in the next lane interrupted my procrastination ritual.

"Are you going to jump in or not?"

That day, I discarded the delay tactics and negative self-talk and chose to live by faith in swimming and all areas of my life: Trusting God when my children left the nest—starting a writing career in my fifties, working through family dysfunction, and speaking in public.

I discovered God delights in giving us the courage and strength we need whenever we take a step of faith. When we do, He's sure to follow with even more assignments.

Nehemiah received a God-sized assignment. He had served as cupbearer for King Artaxerxes and took a leap of faith when he received the news of the destruction of Jerusalem. The city had been left defenseless after years of neglect. Before Nehemiah even approached the king to request a leave, he prayed. The king agreed, clearing the first major obstacle.

Once Nehemiah arrived, forces opposed him. Three men constantly mocked the builders' every move, scoffing at their progress, "Even a fox could jump that wall and break it down. You'll never finish the city's wall. You're pathetic." Nehemiah remained undaunted. He knew the God of heaven would help them succeed.

Nehemiah encouraged the people to keep working. He knew God's work rarely moves forward without resistance. Throughout this opposition, Nehemiah prayed, and God gave the workers "the mind to work."

These four words of scripture became a rallying cry for my life. With God's help, I learned to swim slowly but proficiently across the pool and back. Believe me, I wanted to quit so many times. As I labor on other tasks, I continue to recall this verse. When I do, God renews my strength and courage, no matter how discouraging and toilsome the work.

Whether your assignment from God is a weighty matter or a personal endeavor like swimming the length of a pool, pray and ask God for help. He will give you the will to complete the assigned task.

Prayer

Lord, some days, the task seems weighty and impossible. I wonder if You called the right person for the assignment. Would You give me the will to keep working? I need You, Lord! I trust You to battle my opponents and give me the courage and strength I need to move forward in Your work. In Jesus' name, amen.

Be Strong and Courageous

Lauren Crews

"Only be strong and very courageous; be careful to do according to all the Law which Moses My servant commanded you; do not turn from it to the right or to the left, so that you may achieve success wherever you go." Joshua 1:7 NASB

צְמַאוּ קזח

I have a confession. As a girl growing up, I was a little jealous of boys. When we were on the playground, they could get lost in their imaginations as superheroes fighting for justice to protect the world. I was resigned to being the damsel in distress who needed saving, but I wanted to be in on the action! Ribbons and bows didn't appeal to me. I wanted to be strong and courageous.

Growing up in Sunday school, I learned of Shadrach, Meshach, and Abednego's bravery in facing the fiery furnace; David's courage in bringing down a giant; and Joshua's fearless military exploits. But, again, they're guys. What's a girl to do? I could find biblical examples of women like Deborah, who was a leader, and Esther, who proved a woman could be beautiful and wise, but where was my superheroine of courage and strength?

God used the words of Joshua 1:7 uniquely and extraordinarily in my life. Its phrase, "be strong and courageous," beckoned me to overcome great fear of the unknown and plunge into a new career. These words reminded me how He has overcome the back story of my life, and He released me from the captivity of shame and doubt. He still uses the phrase to encourage me when I want to retreat instead of facing the difficult parts of life.

Fundamentally, to be strong means to have physical and mental power. To be courageous is to be characterized as bold. But there's more. Sometimes when God uses particular words in the Bible, He builds an extra measure of understanding into those words, so we know how to apply them to our lives. Often, we need this extra dose of understanding, especially when our confidence is shrinking and fear becomes oppressive.

"Be strong and courageous."

I love these words so much I had them tattooed on my arm in Hebrew. When people ask me what they mean, I always respond, "Do you want to know what it says or what it means?"

You see, there is a difference. The Hebrew letters are more than sounds strung together to make words. Each letter holds a pictograph—a word picture—and God uses these pictures to add another layer of meaning. The pictures related to each letter in the word *strong* give us insights into God's deeper connotation.

Strong, in Joshua 1:7, is spelled in Hebrew with three letters—chet, zayin, and qof. The dimension God adds to each letter is striking:

ח – Chet—a protective fence or wall. It holds the idea of being surrounded by protection.

ז – Zayin—a sword which is a defensive weapon we use when we take action.

46

ק – Qof—the back of the head. It refers to something behind us.

Courageous is spelled in Hebrew with four letters:

ו – Vav—a nail. It is the conjunction *and* in Hebrew. It represents being attached.

א – Alef—an ox. It represents strength and is a Hebrew symbol for God.

מ – Mem—water. It can also mean chaos. We get this idea from rushing water.

צ – Tzade—a fishhook. It can represent being pulled away in captivity.

When we include the pictograph meaning of the words, "be strong and courageous," they become more than just an idea of physical and mental power and boldness. God adds why we can be strong and courageous and how. Read the phrase with the included word picture meanings:

Be strong—You are enclosed within My wall of protection. I am your refuge. I am with you as you take up your sword. I AM the Word. I AM the sword of the spirit. Walk before Me. I have your back.

And courageous—Attach, nail yourself, to God's strength so when you face chaos, which can overcome you like rushing water, you will not be hooked and carried away.

Now that is strength and courage! When we know the depth of God's word, we can appreciate the depth of His love and care for us. When we experience His love for us, we can trust Him more and be strong and courageous as He desires us to be. It forms an awe-inspiring circle that develops holiness in our lives.

Prayer

Lord, the encouragement of strength You provide in Your word is uplifting and inspiring. Abba, Father, we confess we often need reminding to embrace Your courage, so we won't have to be frightened or dismayed. We know that the purest strength comes from embracing Your character and becoming more like you. You never fail, and You are always with us wherever we go. In Jesus' name, amen.

Simple Courage

Tracy Crump

"Be strong and courageous. Do not fear or be in dread of them, for it is the LORD your God who goes with you. He will not leave you or forsake you." Deuteronomy 31:6 ESV

C haperoning a group of teens at our state's annual youth convention kept me busy, so I looked forward to free time one afternoon when we would unwind for a bit doing crafts. That's where I first noticed Jenny checking out available projects. It was hard not to notice her. As she milled about the room with other teens, her limbs jerked unpredictably. Even when she tried to stand still, muscle spasms seized an arm and threw it into the air or wrenched her head to the side. Kids would glance up in surprise and then look away quickly. My heart ached to see how cerebral palsy affected her life.

Before long, Jenny settled on a wood-burning project and began gathering her supplies. Since I was never good at artistic endeavors, it didn't matter which craft I chose, so I sat across from her. I picked up a thin wood plank and penciled my last name on it with a little flower in the corner. That was the extent of my creative abilities. Meanwhile, Jenny sketched intently on her plaque. Curious, I turned my head so I could see what she drew. A handsome cardinal sat on a branch surrounded by dogwood blooms.

"Pretty," I said.

She smiled.

I picked up the hot tool to begin. How would Jenny complete her project without burning herself? She didn't. I winced each time her spastic movements elicited another "Ouch!" But under Jenny's hands, a beautiful image took shape.

Dutifully searing my name into my piece of wood, I struck up a conversation. "What county are you from?"

"Pontotoc." Even her voice quivered from the effects of her disorder.

"That's not too far from us. What project area are you in?"

"Clothing."

"Oh, do you sew?" I marveled that she could control her hands enough to do such intricate work.

Her bright eyes looked straight into mine. "I sew some, but I'm here to compete in the clothing selection contest. We coordinate outfits from clothes we buy at the store. I'll model my outfit this evening at the general assembly."

Model? Several youths had made rude noises and hurled insults at talent contest participants the night before. Was she going in front of that group? They would eat her alive!

I gave her my best encouraging smile. "I'll watch for you."

Later that day, I entered the auditorium with trepidation, remembering Jenny. After everyone sat down, the lights dimmed, and clothing selection contestants lined up on the stage. I could pick out Jenny even at that distance. She stood in the model's pose just like the other girls, but her head or arm occasionally twitched involuntarily.

When it came time for Jenny to walk the "runway," I held my

breath. The teens had clapped politely for the other contestants, but what would they do when Jenny lurched across the stage? A burned finger might be pleasant compared to this. I felt as nervous as if I were the one going in front of all those people with so little control over my body. Would I have found the courage to do it? I closed my eyes and prayed as my new friend took her first few steps in front of over six hundred of her peers.

For a moment, there was deadly silence. Then the entire audience broke into thunderous applause. Tears streamed down my cheeks as I clapped, too.

Cerebral palsy may have controlled Jenny's movements, but it didn't control her life. With quiet courage, she demonstrated what she could accomplish with a positive attitude. Drawing, sewing, modeling? No problem. All you need to do is try. Whether her body cooperated or not, Jenny was determined to be happy doing the things she loved.

From that day forward, I stopped thinking about what I couldn't do and focused on what I could. Following Jenny's example, I've walked a few runways I wouldn't normally have attempted and found happiness waiting at the end.

Sometimes courage is putting one foot in front of the other.

Prayer

Jesus, you faced crowds of people, some of whom hated You, but You did it anyway to bring them the good news. Though life is hard sometimes, hiding from challenges won't accomplish anything. Only by stepping out and calling on You, Jesus, for help can we find the courage to make a difference in this world. Please gift me with wisdom, courage, and strength. In Jesus' name, amen.

What Now?

Sharon Davis

*"Then Samuel took a stone and set it up between
Mizpah and Shen. He named it Ebenezer, saying, 'Thus
far the LORD has helped us.'" 1 Samuel 7:12 NIV*

I've thought and prayed about it, and I've decided to take the severance package." I gulped. There. It was out. Relief and fear fought for control of my heart.

Silence.

"Well, okay. That wasn't what I was expecting to hear," said my district manager.

It wasn't what I expected I'd be saying, either. Who was this person leaving the security of a good job for the unknown? Didn't sound like me. A smart woman with a plan mapped out in her head for the next five to eight years, wouldn't leave her job. Single and fifty-eight years old, I had sole responsibility for the upkeep of my household. What was I thinking? The new job they offered was a little different in some aspects, but doable. So, why didn't I take it?

Needing to see the whole picture when I made the decision, I did what I always do; I made a list. In one column, I listed

53

the reasons to stay. In the other, the reasons to leave. The stay column was a lot longer. But as I prayed and read the list, God showed me what surrender to Him looked like for me. It was total surrender. Something I found I had never really done.

My whole life I had dreamed of becoming a published author. One of those impossible dreams you can't quite grab hold of because life gets in the way. A dream you make excuses for not following. Promising myself I would wholeheartedly pursue the dream once I retired and had more time. I would work at my safe job, hopefully for the next few years, and then I would go for the dream.

Sometimes God gives you what you ask for, but in ways you never thought. He gave me time. Exactly what I needed. Completely opposite of the way I thought I would get it. God's like that. He knew I needed to know for certain that this time was from Him and not something I had provided. Now, I had to decide whether or not to take it or to continue on in my own strength.

Leaving would mean trusting God, and only God, with my future. Reading and rereading my list, I knew in my soul He was calling me to surrender all my plans to Him. He showed me the main difference in the two columns had to do with trust. The stay column was trust in what I could provide. The go column was all about God. It became the obvious choice to go with God. A weight lifted from my soul, and He gave me peace.

Even so, I wore out my pillow and finished a bottle of antacids in those three days of decision making. Not because I didn't trust His hand, but because I had trusted my own hand for so long.

Giving up control of my life, whether I really had it or not, was like wrenching a sore tooth from a clenched jaw.

Once I made the decision known, confirmation came from unexpected directions. The severance package terms ended up being way more money than I was told. A very welcome surprise. Next, having worked with the same company for so many years, I had loads of unused sick time and paid time off. I was told I would lose all that. After talking with the HR person, I found out I would be able to cash in most of that time before I finished working out my notice. Also, I discovered my medical insurance could be continued. Blessing after blessing poured in when I chose to trust God's plan. Why did I ever want to trust in myself?

Knowing my penchant for self-doubt and second-guessing, I wrote down the experience and all the things I perceived God telling me. Six months down the road, I was likely not to remember all the details and the confirmation in my soul of God's path. Sure enough, the farther from the encounter with God, the less I remembered His hand in all of it. I returned to my account several times whenever doubt threatened to derail me. Like the stone set up in remembrance by Samuel when God helped the Israelites defeat the Philistines, I had my own Ebenezer to help remind me of God's help.

Whenever God leads you to follow His direction, write it down. Make your own Ebenezer stone. That way, when doubt sneaks back in, you have a solid reminder of God's help. Live in His confidence.

Prayer

God, please give me the boldness to follow Your calling and help me to carry it out. I don't want to miss any of Your goodness You have for me. Thank You for being the giver of good, good gifts. In Jesus' name, amen.

Just Pray:
Lessons From a Little One

Dawn Marie Day

*"Cast your burden upon the LORD and He
will sustain you" Psalm 55: 22A NASB*

Have you felt fearful? Anxious? Overwhelmed? Burdened? Of course, you have. We all have at one time or another throughout our lives. Most of the time, we think we can take care of our problems, or we turn on the TV and try to forget they exist until we start to feel a pressing weight from all sides.

I was recently feeling fearful about upcoming changes in my job and some decisions I had to make that would impact my life significantly. I typically don't dwell on things to the point of feeling burdened, but this time, a tinge of anxiety settled in as my mind waded through the mire of thoughts clouding my brain. But just as the anxiety rose to a level of fear, an important lesson a grandson taught me came to mind.

A few years ago, I had taken my grandsons, Luca, Elijah, and Isaiah, to the beach house we rented at the time. I often took the boys for a fun weekend in the sun and some Nana-and-boys time. That first night, I tucked them in as usual after popcorn and a movie. Isaiah, the baby, slept alone in one bedroom so the older boys wouldn't disturb him. Luca and Elijah usually shared the second bedroom with me. We would read books and snuggle until the boys settled, then I would go to the living room to recoup after a busy day.

On this particular night, Luca, the eldest of the three, fell asleep soon after reading about how Splat the Cat went to the beach to collect some seashells for show and tell. But Elijah, then three years old, was still awake, and as I tried to leave, he called me back into the room.

"Nana," he said, "I'm scared."

I gently reassured him I would be in the next room, and everything would be okay. I hugged him and stood to leave.

"But, Nana, I'm scared."

Again, I sat next to him, kissed him, and told him I would leave the hall light on for him. As I walked out of the room, I heard, "Nana, I'm really scared."

For the third time, I sat next to him, hugged and kissed him, and assured him there was nothing to fear. This time as I rose from the bed, his soft, sweet voice said, "But, Nana, will you just pray for me?"

There they were. Six words. The most beautiful six words I had heard from this little one's mouth. "Will you just pray for me?" He didn't want me to kiss him again, tell him everything would be okay, leave the light on, or even sit close by in the next room. That precious little boy just wanted me to pray away his fear.

So, I prayed with Elijah that night. Together we asked God to take away Elijah's fear, help him sleep well, and wake him refreshed and ready to serve God the next day. We also prayed for Luca and Isaiah, then I kissed him goodnight one more time.

Well, don't you know, as I walked out of the room, I looked back at my sweet Elijah—who was sound asleep. Peace had enveloped him immediately, and he rested perfectly in God's arms that night.

As I reflected on the lesson God taught me through a three-year-old boy, I was convicted. I had allowed the weight of decisions and uncertainties to wreak havoc on my emotions instead of casting them on God's shoulders through a simple little prayer. Once I handed over each concern, each little tinge of anxiety, and every burden surrounding my work situation to Jesus, I felt an overwhelming calm rush over me. I will never forget the feeling of weight being lifted from me, as if God had reached down and set me on a cloud.

At only three years old, Elijah knew the most basic things. Prayer is powerful. Prayer removes fear. Prayer heals. Prayer is better than a kiss goodnight or a light left on in the hallway. God hears us. He wants us to seek Him in the midst of our troubles.

Just like David wrote in Psalm 55:22, we can cast our "burdens on the Lord and He will sustain us." We can pile our worries, fears, and anxieties on the Almighty's shoulders. He will give us peace and rest and hold us up through it all.

But we have to trust that promise. Do you? As Christians, our role is to do what God has called us to do, not to be weighed down with worry and fear. Don't waste another minute holding on to the cares of this world. Let God hold your burdens so He can sustain you for the life He has purposed for you.

Prayer

Abba, please remind me as soon as a situation occurs to pray and to bring all my worries, concerns, and decisions to

You. You are able and willing to carry my burdens. Thank You for loving me even when I delay in coming to You with my cares and joys. You are a good Father indeed. In Jesus' name, amen.

My Sinai Saga

Jarm Del Boccio

*"Since you are my rock and my fortress, for the sake of
your name lead and guide me." Psalms 31:3 NIV*

I was hoping for a full moon to give us light, but it was pitch black when Mohammed, our English-speaking Bedouin guide, met us. He led us to where we would mount our Sinai Desert camels for the hour and a half ride. It would take us two-thirds of the way to the summit. I was struggling with "Pharaoh's revenge" and arthritic knees, so I breathed a prayer, asking God to stay my infirmities so I could complete the much-anticipated nocturnal journey.

Though we were using our flashlights, we could barely see the path beneath our feet, but we could hear the camel drivers shouting orders in Arabic from every direction. Their words seemed to bounce off the surrounding mountains and echo across the hillside. Soon the camels came into view, bathed by a glow of yellow light, rounded up and ready to escort us up the mountain. Their musky odor was memorable.

My daughter, Olivia, and I were chosen first to mount our camels and lead the group. We remembered to lean back when our beast of burden made his two-step maneuver to stand. Forward, then backward, and up we went.

I was told to move ahead, so, with a swat and click of the tongue from a Bedouin child, we were off: clippity, cloppity, clop, moving in a slow rhythmical stride, in rocking horse fashion. Where we were going, I did not know. Since I couldn't see the ground, or even a hand in front of my face, I raised my head to the sky. And what I saw took my breath away.

Because there was no moon, millions upon millions of stars were visible in the night sky. The twinkling bodies that dotted the heavens seemed to wink at me, as if they held a magnificent secret that would be revealed. For the first time, I realized the sky was alive.

And then I saw it. A shooting star. I gasped with delight, ready to share my discovery, but I realized my trusty camel had moved ahead of the group, leaving me alone. During the remainder of the trek, I counted ten of them; more than I had seen in a lifetime. All because I had kept my eyes on the heavens. I began to quietly sing, "I just keep trusting my Lord as I walk along…tho' the storm clouds darken the sky on the heavenly trail…I just keep trusting my Lord, He will never fail. He's a faithful friend…I can count on Him to the very end." Even though I am fearful of heights and could not see the outer edge of the trail leading up the mountainside, I was not afraid.

It occurred to me I often find myself worried about the road ahead when God (like the camel) knows the path intimately. If I had relaxed and looked up to Him, I would have had numerous blessings to enjoy. Instead, I was focused on my fears.

I thought of God's promise to Abraham that his descendants would be as inestimable as the sands below his feet and as innumerable as the stars in the heavens above him. As I lifted my eyes to the nighttime sky, I could see Orion's Belt, and soon after, the Big Dipper, standing on its handle. And, stretched across the expanse was the Milky Way. An awesome sight.

Since I was traveling well ahead of the other twelve in our party, with no one leading me, I had the sky and trail to myself for almost an hour. At one point, I glanced behind me and noticed a zigzagged path of sojourners on foot, their lights flickering in the night as they made their way to the summit. Our lives are like a pilgrimage, I thought. We take a step at a time as God gives us light for our paths, always moving forward.

Our ride came to an end far too soon. My buddy, the Sinai Desert camel, had taken me to my destination safely. I was ready to meet the remainder of our group to walk the final two hours to the summit, anticipating the beautiful sunrise. Our Bedouin guide, who also knew the path well, brought us to the top just in time to see the sun break on the horizon. The craggy rocks surrounding us, and as far as the eye could see, changed to various shades of orange and brown as the ball of fire rose in the sky. We heard pilgrims singing hymns of praise to God, their hands outstretched to the heavens, and felt an awe-inspired hush as we continued to witness the majesty and creativity of our Savior.

As we walked down the mountain in the morning sun, I noticed our trail was covered with stones. Most of them were large and uneven, making our descent on foot difficult. But being carried by the camel while going uphill was a smooth experience. It was quite an unexpected discovery. His large sprawling feet took the bumps for me. Again, when I left the journey to the One who knew the way, the uphill climb was almost effortless. And my prayers had been answered throughout the journey. My knees did not pain me, nor was I bothered by Pharaoh's revenge. Another little miracle to remind me of God's faithfulness.

It was a never-to-be-forgotten experience in which I learned to trust in God and His direction for my life. And I've fallen in love with my Sinai Desert camel. Thanks for the ride. And the lessons!

Prayer

Thank you, Lord, for being there beside me during difficult times, bearing me up and making rough places level. In Jesus' name, amen.

With or Without Tears

Becky Hitchcock

"Therefore I remind you to stir up the gift of God which is in you." 2 Timothy 1:6a NKJV

We were at the closing service of a women's retreat when the director whispered, "Your sensitivity is a gift."

I beamed with gratitude but wondered why Gaile noticed me. Even though I'd served as a retreat team member, I hadn't been a speaker and had kept a low profile throughout the entire weekend.

Yet this wasn't the first time someone had described me as sensitive. Growing up I'd heard the word, along with "too tenderhearted," spoken in hushed tones by family and teachers. And it always felt strange that they were talking about me because I seldom cried—the true mark of a sensitive person. Or so I thought. In my early years I learned that bursting into tears over every disappointment would make people say I was spoiled. My daddy used to say, "I don't have any spoiled children." Daddy held fast to the philosophy that he couldn't spoil a baby by loving it. Indeed, I was very loved. So I didn't want anybody telling my daddy I was spoiled.

Yet, even without tears, within the measure of a moment, I could feel a myriad of things. Tender and deep things. Things that slipped into lingering thoughts I seldom shared with anyone. And so, I took for home that day with a new spring in my step. No one had ever told me God made me sensitive on purpose—that it was an actual gift.

A multitude of remarks have since passed my way. Yet Gaile's words stay with me because they stir a gift. A gift that had lain dormant and unrealized for many years. So I treasure her words. I ponder them perpetually with the Scriptures. And whenever I ponder the Scriptures about anything, I learn many things.

Yet, it's a bona fide truth: my feelings still run deep and tender. They're easily stung and, if left unchecked, will produce a domino-style effect in my soul. With or without tears, hurt feelings will form into an offense. They will shape into self-pity, then resentment. And then, in no time at all, a root of bitterness springs up (Hebrews 12:15). And so, I'm learning not to rehearse hurt feelings by holding them close in my thoughts or by venting them to whomever will listen (Proverbs 29:11).

"A person's wisdom yields patience; it is to one's glory to overlook an offense" (Proverbs 19:11 NIV).

The key word is *learning*. Not learned. Overlooking an offense is quite a challenge. But taking an offense requires no talent; it's too common to be a gift. Moreover, taking an offense doesn't bring glory to the God who created me to be sensitive and not to reek of bitterness. So I hold Gaile's words close in my thoughts. I rehearse them, so to speak, with the Scriptures, especially when my feelings have been stung.

"Let all bitterness…be put away from you…And be kind to one another, tenderhearted, forgiving one another, even as God in Christ forgave you. …And walk in love, as Christ also has loved us and given Himself for us, an offering and a sacrifice to God for a sweet-smelling aroma" (Ephesians 4:31, 32; 5:2 NKJV).

And there are other words I rehearse—words learned from a co-worker. When I worked with John we often talked about the loved ones we each had to bury. Another bona fide truth is that I learned too early in life about death and funerals. Yet John's loss is the greater; he buried a son. John gave me a prayer card from his church. The card is penned with words from Francis of Assisi:

"Lord, make me an instrument of your peace; where there is hatred, let me sow love; where there is injury, pardon; where there is doubt, faith; where there is despair, hope; where there is darkness, light; and where there is sadness, joy. O Divine Master, grant that I may not so seek to be consoled as to console; to be understood as to understand; to be loved as to love. For it is in giving that we receive; it is in pardoning that we are pardoned; and in dying that we are born to eternal life."

Gaile's remark and John's prayer card are treasures from decades ago. These treasures stir a gift. A gift I continue to ponder with the Scriptures so I continue to learn many things. So far, I've learned that, with or without tears, spoiled and sensitive are not the same. Moreover, I've learned that God created me sensitive on purpose for the sake of others: to see their sufferings as greater than my own. And to better realize my own great need for Him.

For surely, it's the greatest need I have—the most bona fide truth I know.

Prayer

Father, stir the gift You placed within me so others may know You, and to better understand my own great need for You. In Jesus' name, amen.

My Name Meant "Ugly"

Lollie Hofer

"And he brought him to Jesus. Now when Jesus looked at him, He said, 'You are Simon the son of Jonah. You shall be called Cephas.' (which is translated, A Stone)." John 1:42 NKJV

God doesn't always see you as others see you. He sees qualities in you others might overlook.

Petros? A rock? Jesus called Simon immovable and steadfast? Those acquainted with Simon were probably shocked at his new name. They knew him all too well… hot-headed, impetuous, and reactionary. Those traits, a part of his character, surfaced on numerous occasions throughout the gospels.

At birth, I had wrinkled red skin and bright red curly hair. Mother enjoyed showing me off but for the wrong reasons. She said people would peek into the baby buggy and gasp, "Oh my!" She found their reactions hilarious.

My grandfather called me Lollipop because he said I looked like a red sucker. At two weeks of age, the *pop* was dropped, and I've been Lollie ever since. For years whenever people asked me what my name meant, I responded "Ugly."

As a child, I experienced major rejections resulting in extreme insecurities. Mother's story simply reinforced the reality of my ugly life.

I never met my father face-to-face. My sister, Dee, was four months old when I was conceived. My father felt he couldn't afford another child as a low-income sailor stationed in Washington, D.C. He wanted Mother to abort me, although abortions were illegal in the 1950s.

For several reasons, including protecting my life, she left him. She caught a ride on a military bus headed to Chicago, Illinois. Her parents, from Macomb, Illinois, met her and Dee at the naval base and took them to their home.

My father never came to get his family or to see me. Their divorce finalized when I was four months old. From a child's perspective, I assumed he rejected me because I was an unlovely child.

Mother remarried when I was five, and I wanted my stepfather to adopt me. A few years later, at a birthday party for him, I planned the perfect gift (or so I thought). I made an adoption certificate with my last name changed to his. I gave him the gift in front of about thirty people. "Adopt you?" he asked. He ripped the certificate to shreds. "I'd be embarrassed to have you as a daughter."

My heart shattered beyond repair, and after that I stayed in the shadows where I belonged. I tried not to draw attention to myself. And I never saw fulfilled the one thing I desired the most…the unconditional love of a father.

Once I became a Christian, I still clung to the idea I couldn't be loved. That is until Abba Father danced with me and ministered to the emotional wounds I carried.

One Sunday evening an evangelist spoke at our church. I don't remember what she spoke on; I do remember the wor-

ship. Until then, I never went forward to the altars to partici-
pate in worship. I enjoyed those things but usually held back. I
never felt worthy enough to join in.

Sensing the nudge of the Holy Spirit, I went forward. I
moved to the far-right corner of the altar area where I wouldn't
bring attention to myself. I stood in a corner, my back to the
others gathered there.

As I worshiped, I became aware of the tangible presence of
God. He took my breath away.

In a vision, I sensed the Father wanted to take my hand and
dance with me. I hesitated. He reached for my hand anyway.
Later, folks told me they were surprised to see conservative
me dancing in the corner, although they discerned perhaps, I
wasn't dancing alone.

"I AM your Daddy-God," He said as we twirled and
laughed. "I'm the Father you've longed for. I never saw you
as ugly. Your name means compassionate daughter, and I'm
proud to be your Pappa."

Healing began as I saw myself through His eyes.

Unlike Simon, only the meaning of my name changed. Jesus completely changed Simon's to Cephas in Aramaic (Peter
in Greek) which is translated a stone or rock. As in a large
boulder. Immovable. Strong. Steadfast.

God sees in us what we can't see in ourselves. As a result
of insecurities, I struggled to look beyond "ugly" to see who I
had become…a godly woman full of compassion. My heavenly Father did see the true me. He also saw in Peter who he was
to become. Through the inward work of the Holy Spirit, Peter
turned into a powerful, stabilizing leader in the New Testa-
ment church.

Soon after that night, I began to study Scriptures to learn
who I am in Christ. The verses strengthened my faith to be-

lieve that I indeed had a purpose and value. He transformed me by renewing my mind (Romans 12:1, 2).

It was important for me to change my perception of myself. As long as I believed the worst about me, Satan had the upper hand. He was intent on my destruction and to steal my effectiveness in God's kingdom. However, God desired to give me abundant life through His Son, Jesus Christ (see John 10:10).

I had a choice: Believe the lies or believe the truth. Through persistent study of who I am in Christ, I chose to believe God.

Do you struggle to see yourself as God sees you? You, too, can choose to believe His truth instead of Satan's lies. Ask God to show you who you are in Him. Give the Holy Spirit permission to do an inward healing work. And study His Word. It will set you free (see John 8:31, 32).

Prayer

My God, my God, you see me for who I truly am. You created me in the image of You, and I am beautiful because you fearfully and wonderfully created me. Please help me see myself the way You see me. Heal me and allow me to hear and trust You. In Jesus' name, amen.

No Regrets

Penny Hunt

"Come now, you who say, 'Today or tomorrow we will
go into such and such a town and spend a year there
and trade and make a profit'—yet you do not know
what tomorrow will bring." James 4:13–14a ESV

Have you ever made excuses for not doing the good you knew you ought to do?

One of the lesser sacrifices military wives make is how move-after-move we leave behind the gardens we've lovingly planted and cared for. And even more difficult is our sacrifice of leaving behind the friends we've made.

The saying, "Absence is to love as wind is to fire—it extinguishes the small and enkindles the great," certainly rings true regarding friendships that have begun and ended with a change of duty stations.

Even with today's technology, it's easy to lose contact with friends from the past, and over time, distance loses the closeness once shared. This happened when we left Hawaii. My next-door neighbor, who had seen me through post-operative recovery while my husband was deployed, hid bicycles in her garage until Christmas eve and helped me plant Hawaiian ginger in the backyard.

Over time we connected less and less, sending only the occasional card and holiday newsletter. I thought of her often, especially when I pulled out a favorite recipe and saw her name in the space designated "from the kitchen of." But new friends in new places with new gardens and responsibilities required most of my time and energy. Now and then, I'd pick up the phone and give her a call, but catching up long-distance was never the same as seeing her face-to-face. Little by little, the phone calls became fewer until they eventually stopped altogether.

When word reached me that she was suffering from a life-threatening disease, I called again, listened to her voice's frailty, and was saddened to hear how much she was enduring. I prayed and sent funny "thinking of you" and elegant get-well cards with notes of encouragement. When God impressed me with the thought to visit her, I said yes in my heart, and meant it, but each time I made plans, something came up, and I didn't go.

The prompting of "Go visit Lynn" returned often, and just as often, I put it off with a list of excuses for not immediately obeying what God told me to do. Lynn died before I ever visited.

Sometime later, I was asked to speak at a church near where Lynn had lived, and on my way home, I stopped by to see her husband. Charlie greeted me warmly and was so kind and understanding as I apologized for not having come sooner. "Oh," he said, "don't worry. I know Lynn would have loved it—but I understand. You're a very busy lady, and we live far away." We both cried as he shared Lynn's end-of-life story and laughed, remembering some of the crazy things we'd done together.

As our visit came to its natural conclusion, Charlie asked if I had time to see where he did his woodworking. "Of course," I said and followed him to what I expected would be a rustic carpenter shop with a table or chair in the making. It was a surprise to instead find a studio displayed with stunning works of art he'd created from burl wood.

Unfamiliar with burl wood, I was fascinated to learn they were the ugly knots formed on tree trunks and are greatly prized by woodcarvers for their inner beauty. Charlie showed me the carving tools and grinders he used and some of the pieces he'd recently fashioned. When he stopped me and insisted I accept a necklace he'd made that reminded me of a wooden tear, I gratefully accepted it and was on my way.

Not long after my return home, I came across this poem:

> Oh, my friends, it would be better
> If to those we love, we gave
> Tender words while they were living
> Then to say them over the grave.
> Anonymous

Tears of regret stung my eyes at the first reading of those words. But later, remembering the necklace Charlie had given me, a thought I often share with others came to mind. "Keep the lesson and let go of the pain."

I prayed again, confessing my disobedience and adding thanksgiving for the lesson God had taught me. At that moment, His grace and love turned what had been an ugly knot of guilt and self-reproach into a deeper understanding of the blessings He has in store when I willingly and quickly obey the promptings of His Holy Spirit.

Prayer

Sovereign Lord, help us live in attentive obedience to Your will and ways, immediately responding to whatever You ask us to do. Please let me keep the lessons you have for me and let go of the pain. In Jesus' name, amen.

Right Where God Is

Mary-Anne Rubado Kline

*"I lift my eyes to the hills. From where does my help come? My help comes from the L*ORD*, who made heaven and earth." Psalm 121:1–2 ESV*

Do you have an object you look at in amazement? Is it something you seek refuge in? For me it is the glorious Rocky Mountains. When I moved to Colorado in 2005, I was enamored with the beauty of these mountains.

Living in Florida for the first twenty-four years of my life, all I had known were the waves of the ocean as they crashed against the shore. Such a difference in God's creation. I have called Colorado my home for nine years.

Most of my Christ growing, learning, and transforming would take place here, although I would not know it when I arrived. Each morning I get the joy of peering out my bedroom window and seeing the colors of sunrise wash across these majestic mountains. It is like a breath of fresh air telling me God is with me. He sees and knows Mary-Anne.

When the world is heavy, I see those mountains and they steady me. God steadies me. And when I cannot see the mountains because of a snowstorm or rain shower, I am reminded God is still there.

And boy, those mountains have sure seen me in the storms life brings. The death of my first husband, Charlie, had me on my knees more times than I could count, crying out to God. My heart was completely shattered. I did not know what to do next or how to go on living this life without him.

Our home on Fort Carson faced Cheyenne Mountain, so each day I would drag myself out of bed. I would walk our beloved pup, Indiana, or walk with some of my close Army wife friends there on post. Those majestic mountains were in my view. And if I were close enough to them, they would shelter me, providing shade from the sun.

Isn't that exactly what God does? He holds us close and protects us, not always physically, but in spirit and soul, as we remain close to Him. In seeing those mountains, I could keep going through the continued storms of this life knowing God would meet me as I was and be my help. Even when I had no idea what would happen next.

As my life moved forward, I decided to remain in Colorado Springs after my time living on Fort Carson was complete. The mountains were a beacon of hope for me because I knew who made them. God was my refuge. I ran to them often to seek wisdom, discernment, and encouragement.

My help came from God. He is the only reason I could put one foot in front of the other to begin each new day. My hope and delight were in my precious Savior, in whom I trusted. Those first few years after my husband died, I cried out in anguish, in disbelief, and even in fury. Grief can really bring out the best or the most devastating in a person. And I was no different.

I did not always seek God first. I would have one too many glasses of wine and spend money on things I did not need, either to numb the significant heartache or to make myself happy for a few brief hours. Neither worked, as you can imagine. But each day I began again. God wanted more for me while I was still living this life, and His work was not finished.

God was my help meet. He was my husband. Giving God all my burdens, sufferings, and aching heart was the only way to go through the loss of my Charlie. And by looking at those mountains, I knew God was with me, for me, and helping me. Nothing I did made my life any better. But knowing where my help came from made all the difference.

I can count on seeing God through that mountain each day. And when I cannot see the mountain because of a storm brewing, I am reminded He is still there while waiting for the storm to pass. It can be difficult to see God in the seasons of loneliness and waiting. Oh, the waiting. But once the storm is over and the clouds disperse, there are those mountains that never left when it got too hard. They were right in the midst of the storm. Right where God is. Working for my good and His glory.

God has been so sweet to me and has blessed me in more ways than I can express. But that does not mean my life is easy, or the storms of life are gone. Those same mountains that comforted me through Charlie's death were the same mountains that celebrated with me in marrying my kinsman redeemer, Jeremiah, and reassured me when our oldest son, Ethan, was diagnosed with Type 1 Diabetes.

My help came from the Lord. It continues to come from Him. He never leaves me and is with me wherever I go. Praise God! And to this day, I still peer out our bedroom window and remember every time I looked to those mountains as a beacon of hope, knowing God would be my help and save me.

Prayer

God, please show me who You are amid the storms of my life. Draw close to me. I pray, when the hard storms come in life, I will be battle ready in Jesus' name. Equip me, Lord, with the tools I will need today and in the future. May I hide Your word in my heart. In Jesus' name, amen.

Brown Shoes

Rita Klundt

"When pride comes, then comes disgrace, but with humility comes wisdom." Proverbs 11:2 NIV

A fast walker in this busy hospital hallway typically means one of three things:
- Code blue
- Someone's late for a meeting or taken too long for a break
- The cafeteria's almost out of pizza.

For me, right now, it means I've hit "snooze" on my bladder's alarm at least a half dozen times, and I should've taken a potty break thirty minutes ago. Years of working as a surgical scrub nurse, a cardiac nurse, and now as a dialysis nurse have trained my bladder well, but even the best of nursing bladders has a final warning.

I hope no one suspects the real reason for my urgent stride and undignified wide-swinging hips. This is a Level 1 trauma center. People in scrubs are always racing to get somewhere. But my bladder is screaming. If someone hears it, let them have their suspicions.

Hospital staff and visitors clear the middle of the hallway and allow me to create an emergency lane. I consider things like dignity, pride, and persona, but anyone who mocks because of where I'm going, will mock louder if I don't make it. My elbows pull for a full-blown sprint without thought of who might be upset or injured if all the stalls are occupied.

Midway through my mandatory covering-the-seat ritual, I question if today should be an exception and audibly thank God for the utility of elastic-waisted scrub pants. With the same breath, I beg for two additional seconds as I bend my knees to be seated.

Three walls and a door have physically closed me in but allow my mind to think of less crucial issues. This is my stall—no traffic and no more pressure. Ahhh!

"Brown shoes," I say to myself. "I need some new brown shoes."

The pair of loafers in the stall next to mine are exactly the shade of brown I've been wanting. They have that supple and classy look of expensive leather. Italian leather?

My lips move. "Yes, Italian leather."

I've been looking for about a two-inch heel and something a bit more feminine, but I'd be wearing them with slacks. I'm pulling, tucking and putting things in their place when the brown shoes step out of sight. Their enviable impression remains.

I open the door for a second look at that beautiful leather and to ask where I can buy a pair. The brown shoes are poised in front of a sink. The cuffs of a sharply pressed pair of chestnut brown slacks flirt with that Italian leather. I raise my head to admire what must be a lady of style and means.

I miss the first clue—the mid-thigh lab coat. The stethoscope necklace is a newer model of my own. What? The beige shirt buttons on the wrong side. A tie…and a man's cologne?

I want another look at those shoes, but the indignant beady-eyed scowl of a man grabs me through the mirror and holds me there.

My attempt to communicate an apology through the same mirror is met with an open mouth and a condemning grunt.

I wash my hands thoroughly, more thoroughly than I was taught as a surgical scrub nurse.

The man looks at my name badge. I suppose he wants to be sure my name is spelled correctly on the incident report. His shiny badge brags. "M.D." Based on the University of Illinois' graduation date and his baby face, the badge and title are brand new.

He washes and rinses his hands, then repeats. I accept his medical hygiene challenge and do the same. We reach for a paper towel from the same dispenser. He takes two towels. I take three. He relaxes his gaze before taking a third and a fourth paper towel. We dry between our fingers in unison. His eyes are as green as his shoes are brown. Contacts?

His gritting teeth and disdain give me one more sting before we turn and step toward the exit.

Maybe his mother had taught him well, or maybe he wants to pour salt on my wounded pride. Either way, he pulls the door open, steps back, and yields to me.

The international sign is posted nearer my eye level than his.

Women. Engraved and painted red. The stick person wears a skirt.

Humility, the compulsory kind, covers his face. Neither of us speaks, but I try to convey understanding with a smile and a shrug. He follows me into the hallway, and we are step in step for a while. I want to hate both him and his fine leather shoes, but we'll be working together. Plus, he's young, about the age of my son.

For the sake of all mothers, I decide to forgive his arrogance and appreciate the shoes his mother probably paid for.

"Nice shoes," I say, looking straight ahead not wanting to further humiliate.

No acknowledgement.

Then without a buzz or ding from his pager or phone, he picks up his pace to a squirrel-like scurry. An emergency lane opens, and he's gone.

A nurse whom I've known for several years turns to me and says, "I didn't hear a code blue. Did you?"

"No," I say. "But I hear the cafeteria is almost out of pizza."

The first line of a favored old hymn is "Years I spent in vanity and pride." That implies a sin of the past, but the sin of pride is an everyday, lifelong battle for me. The chorus, however, offers a forever answer: "Great mercy, grace that's free and pardons."

I'd rather look down on someone else's sin, but those brown shoes taught me to check the mirror before pointing a finger.

Prayer

God, please bless me with the confidence to offer mercy, grace, and pardon with a smile. I pray the words of Proverbs 11:2 NIV "When pride comes, then comes disgrace, but with humility comes wisdom." May I be filled with humility and wisdom whether I am the one being insulted or the one pointing fingers. In Jesus' name, amen.

Keeping What We Give Away

Cathy Krafve

"Give, and it will be given to you: good measure, pressed down, shaken together, and running over will be put into your bosom. For with the same measure that you use, it will be measured back to you." Luke 6:38 NKJV

How does welcoming others instruct our hearts? By teaching us that we, too, are worthy of welcome.

All of my files were lost! The computer glitch caused a writer's worst nightmare. Frantically searching my emails for attachments, I soon discovered—since I freely share what I write—that those attachments contained copies of everything important to me. But my giant computer fail highlighted the direct correlation between giving and keeping.

Nowhere is keeping what we give away more dramatic than how we welcome others into our lives and hearts. Not long after my computer glitch, I witnessed a breathtaking example of how we only keep what we give away.

When our son was born, my friend Joan showed up one day with a one-of-a-kind baby gift. Imagine my delight when I opened the package and discovered two tiny treasures from among the keepsakes she saved from her sons' nursery.

Her gift remains one of my all-time favorites. She gave me the gift of herself. I cherished the bib and her antique plaque. But only for a short time. Within months, I received a startling phone call.

"Cathy, a fire destroyed Joan's house last night. But everyone is safe."

The scene was surreal. Only a charred, blackened slab remained of her once beautiful two-story home overlooking the lake, a masterpiece of contemporary architecture designed by a colleague of Frank Lloyd Wright. The insurance company made an initial payment immediately. Within days, Joan's family settled into a rental house with a convenient barn out back for storing the sooty remains of her life.

I showed up a few days later with a casserole, the bib, and the plaque.

Joan welcomed me in a tender embrace. Then she toured me through her rental house as though it was an estate. The family heirlooms once gracing her home had been replaced by practical pieces, like desks from Walmart for her sons.

"Can you believe God found us a rental house with a barn in the back to store everything!"

When she opened the big doors to the barn, the pungent smell of charcoal slammed us. Gratefully, she pointed out that she did not have to store the rubber tubs containing the smelly remains of her life inside her rental house. As we applied cleansers to her elegant china to salvage what little remained, she rejoiced, discovering freedom in letting go of material things. Against all odds, with her beautiful home a smoking mess, she proclaimed God as the One who cared for her family.

Joyfully, she shared how God preserved what was important, burning away all else. She was grateful for her family's safety, but God's provision showed up in the small stuff. For instance, the loss of her sons' baby pictures grieved her the most. Fortunately, over the years, Joan extravagantly shared photos of her children with extended family. Literally, the same pictures she gave away came back to her after the fire. Her emotional well-being and joy in that trying moment affected me forever. I learned something valuable from Joan: we only keep what we give away.

The Scriptures remind us again and again—our hearts only keep what we give away. We can have hearts that welcome others by living open, generous, and vulnerable lives. As we joyfully welcome others, we affirm our worthiness, even in our messiest moments. Consequently, we practice welcoming those we love into a rich circle of fellowship, beginning in our hearts.

Welcoming others with a hospitable heart is the best kind of gift. God does the same for us. When we give a welcome to another person, we demonstrate the generous welcome God lavishes on us. We teach our hearts to love with His "good measure, pressed down, shaken together, and running over" kind of love.

Prayer

Dear Good Father, we need You to teach us to welcome again today. We would never burn down our own house. But it's kinda like burning down our life and heart when we reject ourselves and others. What needless destruction! Instead, help us give away the welcome You give us. We want to rest in the worth You give us. Let us welcome, rather than reject, those around us. Let us see each new person You bring into our lives as a valued, welcome addition. Give us patience and energy to love those who seem hard to love. We know we can't give or love more than You, dear Lord. We just want the "good measure, pressed down, shaken together, and running over" kind of love coming from our hearts by Your beautiful Spirit. Bless us now because that is Your heart's desire. In Jesus' name, amen.

No Medal for Mad

DeeDee Lake

"BE ANGRY, AND YET DO NOT SIN; do not let the sun go down on your anger." Ephesians 4:26 NASB

Did you know there is no medal for being mad the longest? That's right. I've searched. I have not found one. It is not an Olympic event nor a Little League sport. Who knew. We all act like it could be one. Often, we proudly announce how long we were mad at our spouse, boss, or parents. As if someone is going to march up and pin a ribbon on us.

Nope. Not going to happen. No medal. No ribbon. No trophy.

So why do we hang on to mad? It doesn't do anything for our health. In fact, the way I understand it, anger causes our blood pressure to rise. (Please do not take this as medical advice. I have absolutely no medical training whatsoever. None. Zip. Nada).

Years ago, a beautiful mentor told me, as a young wife, she would go long periods not speaking to her husband. I could hardly believe her. Her husband was a saint. He was perfect. Okay. Truthfully. I didn't know him when he was young and stupid. Just when he was old and wise.

As my mentor grew in her Christian faith, she learned she was not to hold on to her anger. God doesn't want the sun to go down on our anger because He knows anger is destructive in many ways. Ephesians 4:26b says, "Don't let the sun go down while you are still angry" (NLT). He wanted her to go to someone as soon as possible and work out whatever was causing trouble in the relationship.

She learned she had to stop her destructive behavior. My mentor was hurting her husband, their marriage, and herself. If she waited a week, two days, or ten minutes to resolve their disagreement, it would still need to be resolved, and the same steps would need to be taken. So, why wait? Why spend any more time in frustration and anger than necessary?

That's God's point too. Why wait? Do we just want to be mad? Is it our desire to sit in our fit? Ever watch a two-year-old decide to be mad for some random reason? It's funny until it isn't. We are grown-up versions of that when we refuse to work things out with someone.

My mentor's words and experience changed me that very day. I had a temper from the day I exploded into the world. I was a red-headed, passionate middle-child who grew into womanhood acting the same way without being checked. Yes, God made me all those things, but He also desired for me to have self-control.

As she shared her story, I realized she probably had an idea that my self-check needed to be checked. I had been unfair to my husband. He was and is a very gentle man who seeks harmony in his life, not chaos or upheaval. I've learned a lot from him. He has always been the first to apologize to seek peace. I knew then that I needed to always try to make things right as soon as possible.

I believed that because I was passionate, it was okay to state my opinions, often with volume. And apologies were not in my communication toolbox.

God's Word says, "be angry, but don't sin." Later, I learned another truth about anger. If *I* was involved in my anger, it was probably not the righteous anger God was talking about in Ephesians. Righteous anger helps us to be aware of and defeat evil in this world. It motivates us to repair the damages, change situations, seek resolutions, and make a difference.

As for the *I* situations, you don't have to be the one who caused the problem, but you can be the one who causes the resolution. Relationships are worth the hard conversations. When I had my passionate nature under control and removed the *I* out of my anger, I became much more approachable, and my relationships blossomed.

The truth is, the quicker you deal with misunderstanding, disagreements, arguments, and other relational issues, the easier they are to resolve. I decided to make it a habit to always work it out. I started that very day. I started with the small stuff. I learned not to hesitate. My delay kept me unhappy and damaged my relationships. I made the decision that my family, friends, workplace, and I would be known for fighting *for* relationships. For that, I *do* deserve a medal!

Prayer

Father God, we are guilty of sins of omission and commission. Your Son died so we may be forgiven of our sins. Please, show, teach, and guide us on how to forgive others. May we forgive and not hold grudges against others as they sin and cause pain. Abba, may we always see people through Your eyes. In Jesus' name, amen.

What Forgiveness Looks Like

Esther Lovejoy

"[A]s the Lord has forgiven you, so you also must forgive." Colossians 3:13b ESV

It wasn't one particular thing, but a lot of deep hurts and frustrations. My reactions felt justified. The other person had truly wronged me multiple times. And yet, I knew the right thing to do. I knew forgiveness was to be my choice, even when it wasn't my emotional preference. I also knew my relationship with the Lord was too important to allow these hurts to hinder that relationship. In fact, my relationship with God was my only hope in this difficult decision. And so, I chose to take the steps toward forgiveness.

It seemed to me the best thing was to make a list—to write down the specifics of what had been done to cause my deep hurt and anger. And so, I did. It wasn't a long list, but it was an honest list. It was a list that contained valid reasons for the pain I was feeling. It was a list that to many, would justify my right to hold this person accountable. I intended to pray through that list, item by item, to make sure my heart was right—and to forgive.

I don't remember what happened, but for some reason, an interruption made it impossible for me to deal with the list right then. I folded the paper and put it in a zippered compartment in my purse so others wouldn't find it. I would get to it as soon as possible.

But the as-soon-as-possible didn't happen. What did happen was that I would take the list out from time to time and review it. I would remember all the valid reasons for my hurt and anger. No doubt it was justified, and I had the list to prove it.

It wasn't long before the Lord began to convict me. I knew rather than using the list to forgive, I had begun to cherish it as a justification for my bitterness. And so, the day came when, in an act of obedience, I once again took the list from my purse and got down on my knees to allow God to do His work of forgiveness in my heart.

It wasn't easy. It wasn't a quick over-and-done-with prayer. This was an honest time in the presence of a holy God as He reminded me that the reasons for forgiveness far outweighed what I believed were justifiable reasons to hold onto my hurt. I stood before God, forgiven. That alone was reason enough. But I also loved God and knew obedience was part of that love. The other person wasn't asking for forgiveness. My guess is they didn't feel the need. It was God who was asking me to forgive. And that was what mattered.

And so, I went down the list. I prayed over each item. I made a choice to truly forgive every wrong, every hurt, every unfair or unreasonable act. I chose to forgive. It wasn't easy, but it was an act of deliberate obedience to the One who loves me and has given His life for me.

And then I had a wonderful idea—an idea I was sure would please God and show Him how sincere I was. I took my list and ripped it up. In a rather dramatic gesture, I tore it to shreds.

Then, in a rather self-righteous act, I dumped it in the trash with a feeling of "So there! Done!" Or so I thought.

Then the Lord spoke. His instructions were clear. I was to get another piece of paper—a blank piece of paper. I was to fold it and put it in the same zippered part of my purse. As I obediently folded up that piece of paper and put it in my purse, I realized God had just shown me a clear picture of what forgiveness truly looks like. Forgiveness is a blank piece of paper.

God, in His wisdom and familiarity with people's hearts, knew that a ripped-up list wasn't enough. He knew there would be times when my old feelings would return—when once again, I would remember those harmful things done against me. In those moments, I needed that blank piece of paper as a visual reminder of my choice to forgive. The list was gone, and a blank piece of paper remained.

Somewhere in heaven, God holds a blank piece of paper as a reminder that I, too, have been forgiven. I know what should be on that list. I know He would be justified to hold those things against me. I know my list would be long. But because of His great love displayed dramatically on a cross, the list is gone. Instead, there is a blank piece of paper—eternal proof that He who asks me to forgive has forgiven much.

Prayer

Father your words in Psalm 139:23–24 NLT are the perfect words for my heart to cry out to you. "Search me, O God, and know my heart; test me and know my anxious thoughts. Point out anything in me that offends you, and lead me along the path of everlasting life." You are my God and the author of my peace through Your wonderful forgiveness. In Jesus' name, amen.

A Dysfunctional Battle Plan Revealed

Carol McCracken

"For the moment all discipline seems painful rather than pleasant, but later it yields the peaceful fruit of righteousness to those who have been trained by it." Hebrews 12:11 ESV

My addiction had caught up with me. This time, I had done it, and I couldn't escape. The assault of flashing blue lights nearly overtook me as I looked through my rearview mirror.

A moment earlier, I realized I shouldn't be driving and pulled over. Too much wine. Again. Feeling my feelings wore me out. Raising a child with special needs and disagreeing with my husband on how to raise our son resulted in an intensely stressful home environment. Rarely did we have a peaceful day.

Choosing to feel nothing rather than something became my coping mechanism. After all, no one would believe what I was going through. And as the Bible study teacher at our church, I had an image to maintain. If my home life wasn't together, it would destroy my credibility with the class. Better not to air dirty laundry.

However, getting numb didn't make the problems go away. A dysfunctional bandage never heals the wound. It simply covers it.

The time had come to face the facts. My judgment was impaired, and the police officer with the flashing blue lights confirmed it. I had a full-fledged addiction, and it had to be dealt with. Past and current family members struggled with alcoholism, but my denial—that it could happen to me—was disproved that night.

Did they not know who I am? My small town was well aware that I am a Bible teacher. Yet even Bible study teachers receive temporarily suspended driver's licenses when they deserve it. Getting used to such an idea took some time. Relying on others to provide my transportation until my court appointment severely injured my pride. The self-reliance I had wrapped around me for so long was snatched away, replaced by an ill-fitting vulnerability. A literal come-to-Jesus meeting followed soon afterward. I distinctly sensed God saying, "We've tried it your way. How's that working for you?"

I surrendered right there, realizing I was unable to heal myself. A twelve-step program was the beginning. And then came my court appearance. I was so nervous, all I wanted to do was hide from the scrutiny. Talk about feeling the feelings. Me, the Bible study teacher, needed to hire a lawyer. The situation left me feeling worthless and dreadfully remorseful.

Then the judge asked me to stand up. He looked at me and told me since I had never done anything like this before, I was never to do anything like it again. He released me with a ticket. There were no further ramifications other than having the literal hell scared out of me. God and this earthly judge gave me another chance, a chance not deserved, and I was not going to blow the opportunity. I had some work to do, so I did it.

My healing began after confessing to my Bible study class. I stood in front of them expecting disapproval or outright condemnation, but the opposite of what I expected happened. Respect not earned came my way. And learning that "acting as if I had it all together" was not authentic ministry, changed me.

Through professional help and hard work, God rewarded me by removing my cravings for alcohol. I had tried many times to stop drinking by using self-discipline. Some people may never understand how addiction makes that impossible. But those who are addicted do. An addiction is a very selfish thing and can scramble an otherwise intelligent person's thinking. I'm always just a drink away from surrendering to addiction's control. But realizing that pearl of wisdom and leaning on Jesus, who is the One in control, provides me with a peaceful, happy life.

The added benefit is that God has allowed my testimony to show how He heals. Life on this earth can be a battle. In the depths of our despair, He invites us to lean on Him to get to the other side of our pain. God sees our hearts. He knows when we're lying to ourselves and others due to inauthenticity. But we don't have to fight the battle on our own.

God gave me a powerful spiritual weapon: His Word. After all, I was teaching it but not applying it correctly. Yes, I prayed. However, choosing self-reliance as my battle plan defeated the purpose. Pride would take me to my knees. But it was also the exact vehicle God used, knowing it would turn me back to His loving arms.

As a loving heavenly Father, God allowed me to experience the consequences of my independent battle plan. He disciplined me as His child. He continues to do so when needed. But it keeps me running back to Him. God knows my stubborn heart because He created me. When I fall, He is there to pick me up. When I tread around in my self-reliant tendencies, He reminds me I am nothing without Him. And what relief this gives me. I don't ever have to fight a battle on my own. And God always wins His battles.

Prayer

Lord, You know me better than I know myself. In my weakness You are strong. My self-reliance can rob me of the joy of seeing You work in miraculous ways. It is through You I find healing. Thank You, Father that through the valleys You still hold me close. In Jesus' name, amen.

Trusting God's Way

Alice H. Murray

*"'For my thoughts are not your thoughts, neither are your
ways my ways,' declares the* Lord.*" Isaiah 55:8 NIV*

The story's ending was great—better than I could have
written. And why not? The Author of the Universe
penned it Himself. The beginning, however, rocked
my world and would never have been the way I would have
chosen for events to unfold.

The words, "I'm afraid we can't work together anymore,"
assaulted my ears. What? Was my boss letting me go? Now?

I stood, frozen, contemplating the grenade that had just been
launched into my little world. Could this possibly have come at a
worse time? The practical, handle-it-yourself me contemplated
the scenario. My husband, who had recently retired from the
military, was pursuing a degree to allow him to embark on a second career. Between us, we had four children to feed and clothe.
How would we ever manage without my income from this job?

Then I heard an amazing statement made by a confident
voice. "I don't know how He will do it, but God will provide
for me." Wait! That was *my* voice!

Those words and my swirling emotions were inconsistent. As an attorney, I was experienced in remaining calm and devising a good strategy to assist my clients. But now, I felt a complete lack of control over my life. Following my unexpected job loss, I did the only thing I could. I cried out to God for His help and proceeded to put one foot in front of the other.

Perhaps I could increase the hours I worked at another part-time job. That position, which gave me great satisfaction, was for an attorney who concentrated on adoption cases. I enjoyed it so much I had even remarked that if God let me do anything I wanted, I would handle adoptions full-time.

Though indicating a willingness to accept my request, this attorney expressed skepticism about whether he had enough adoption work to keep me busy full-time. He said I might have to handle some divorce cases in addition to adoptions to take up the slack. No! Anything but those emotionally charged, ugly situations. But what choice did I have under the circumstances? So, I agreed and came to work for him full-time.

I threw my heart into building up our adoption practice. At times I would handle other cases, such as guardianships, bankruptcies, and appeals, but never did I have to take on a divorce case.

My hard work paid off. The adoption practice boomed. During especially busy times, fifty to sixty-hour weeks were not uncommon. When things got hectic, I'd walk into my boss's office and jokingly ask, "Have any divorce cases you want me to work on?" Both of us would then laugh heartily.

Not only did this job benefit me by providing steady income and professional growth, but it also allowed me to be a vital part of the expansion of my family. My sister and her husband struggled with infertility and felt God was leading them to adopt.

After three years of unfulfilled waiting with an adoption agency in her home state, she sought our office's help. God used me as His instrument in matching my sister and brother-in-law with a birth mother who ultimately placed a bouncing baby boy with them. I even saw the baby before they did and was present when he was discharged from the hospital to his new, forever parents.

Over three decades later, my season handling adoptions at that office ended. I was blessed beyond measure to be allowed to do this type of work and make a difference in children's lives. The job opportunity God opened for me, by unexpectedly allowing me to lose a better-paying job, offered me the chance to walk out my faith. James 1:27 in the NIV tells us "Religion that God our Father accepts as pure and faultless is this: to look after orphans and widows in their distress." I found stable and loving homes for little ones whose parents were unable or unwilling to raise them. Adoption work also allowed me to witness, if not in actual words, then by my actions, to the pregnant women who sought my assistance.

I now recognize my employment has been God's story all along. He had a plan for me. I could not see it and would not have believed that losing a job, whose income my family needed, was one of the greatest blessings God could bestow upon me. He lovingly pushed me toward the open door by forcing me to move through it with a job loss. What I would have missed out on if God hadn't been running the show! My plan to remain employed would perhaps have spared me some temporary pain at the cost of long-term blessings.

What have I learned from this life story? Although, we may not and probably won't always understand God's ways, we must trust Him. We don't need to know the details; we just need to know He loves us and always has our best interests at heart. I also know He writes way better stories than I could ever conceive. Thank you, Lord, for doing things Your way and not mine!

Prayer

Thank you, Father, for knowing me better than I know myself. May I always trust You have my life in Your hands and have a great and wonderful plan for me. You are trustworthy and faithful and for that I'm eternally grateful. In Jesus' name, amen.

Be a Flashlight

Cheryl A. Paden

"You are the light of the world. …In the same way, let your light shine before others." Matthew 5:14a, 16a NIV

I cannot remember a time when I did not have a strong sense of God's presence. At age three I attended Sunday school and church with my Grandma Vida, prayed at bedtime, and said grace with the family at meals.

Along the way there were ah-ha moments. As my faith matured, I began to understand words like *sacrifice*, *resurrection*, *salvation* and *God's grace*. There were times when my walk with God was very close and times when my path would not be quite so close. But whatever the circumstance, God never let go of me.

Even though my relationship with Christ was never in doubt, my struggle was to discover God's calling for my life. I felt assured that every Christian had a purpose, but what was mine? In Matthew's gospel, Christ said we are called to be a light to the world. Not could be, might be, or will be, but are called to be the light of the world. I contemplated how that might look for me. There are many different kinds of light.

I knew I did not want to be like a car with its high beams on, blinding the oncoming traffic causing them to turn away. I was too shy to be that outspoken. I experienced my faith in a quiet presence of God—too shy to be a witness with a lot of vibrato, fearful I would only be turned away or overwhelm the listener.

"If I speak in the tongues of men or of angels, but do not have love, I am only a resounding gong or clanging cymbal" (1 Corinthians 13:1 NIV).

It would be easy to be like a porch light left on during the day. Its light is invisible to the world. Spending time only with my Christian friends, women whom I attend church with, or do Bible study or prayer with. But like the porch light that is only on during the day, I would not be providing any light for those walking in darkness.

"The light shines in the darkness" (John 1:5a NIV).

I also did not want to live my life like a timer-light, the light people use when they go on vacation. It turns off or on at regular intervals to fool people into thinking you're at home when in reality you're out. I knew I could not be a pretend Christian, fooling others or even myself. I wanted to be a 24/7 Christian, living out my faith in every area of my life and not only for myself, but for my sons.

"So whether you eat or drink or whatever you do, do it all for the glory of God." (1 Corinthians 10:31 NIV).

As a youth I attended Christian church camp. To walk from the cabin to the mess hall, another cabin, or vespers at night, a camper must use a flashlight. It was extremely important because its light was needed to safely illuminate the dark path. Without it one might get off the trail or trip over an obstacle. One person holding a flashlight can lead others along the correct path safely. I wanted to be like the flashlight. I wanted to strive to be the kind of light that lit not only the correct path for me but helped others find their Christ-led path. Maybe I couldn't see far down the road, but far enough so I would know the next steps to take.

"Your word is a lamp for my feet, a light on my path" (Psalm 119:105 NIV).

Knowing I was too shy to speak in front of others, I picked up my pen and began to write devotionals and later inspirational stories for publication. In this way I could reach out to many people and let my Christ's light be visible. It felt safe and perhaps God could use me to lead others to faith in Him.

But God did not leave me there. He had an even greater plan for my life. He called me out of my comfort zone and into a position of local pastor. Here by God's power, I preached weekly and served as pastor to small congregations for over ten years. I facilitated retreats and taught Bible studies. What I thought was impossible for me was possible for God. I continue to pray God will use me to shine His light, helping others to follow the path Christ has laid out for them.

Prayer

You are gracious, God, and invite each of Your children to help build Your kingdom. Your invitation includes a calling, a mission for all who know You as their heavenly Father. I pray for wisdom for myself and all my brothers- and sisters-in-Christ to know You more and to hear Your voice. And let us be assured You have placed on each of us a calling. In Jesus' name, amen.

Will I Be Next?

Norma Poore

"Do not fear, for I am with you; Do not anxiously look about you, for I am your God. I will strengthen you, surely I will help you, Surely I will uphold you with My righteous right hand." Isaiah 41:10 NASB1995

Ms. Poore, you have pneumonia and need to stay here a few days," the doctor said.

"Gary died today from pneumonia, while on a ventilator." Mom's words, from three days ago, echoed in my mind.

God, where are you? Am I going to die, too?

Tears burned my eyes and fell on the sheets.

"You shouldn't take that medicine. You know what can happen, not to mention all the adverse side effects," my husband said.

I locked eyes with him. We've endured hardships over the forty years since our vows, but this was different.

"Go on home, honey. I'll be fine. I love you," I said. He blew me a kiss and left.

Controversy about medicine, shots, good healthcare, bad healthcare, and people's opinions blazed through my mind like wild fire. The nurses provided a brief reprieve from my stressful thoughts when they came to check on me.

You'll be next, fear taunted.

Unable to calm my anxious thoughts of not being around to help my daughter with her newborn, not being there to support my family, and not seeing my grandchildren grow up, anxiety tightened its grip. I feared not seeing my children and grandchildren or others I love. I wasn't ready to say goodbye.

A sob caught in my throat. Tears cascaded.

Help me, God. I feel so alone.

Sleep faded in and out as thoughts of death and not seeing those I loved again haunted me.

The nurse pushed back the window curtains. Sunshine spilled into my room. With a smile on her face and kindness in her voice, she attempted to cheer me up. But I didn't want to feign cheerfulness; I needed God to do something. Despite my negative attitude, God reminded me of His promises.

Be still and know that I am God. Surely I will help you. Surely I will uphold you with my righteous right hand. The Lord is the one who goes ahead of you. He will not forsake you. Do not fear.

God's words came to mind like an old friend. Memorized Scripture penetrated my brain fog and brought warmth to my soul. My heavenly Daddy reminded me of His love for me.

"Okay, Father, thank You for bringing Your Word to my mind. It's like salve to a wound. I know if I die, You will take good care of my family and heal their broken hearts. You are so good to me. Thank you," I prayed.

I slept well the next three nights and when I went home with oxygen tanks in tow, peace covered me like a warm blanket.

I learned when I can't feel God's presence, to trust His promises.

Whether you face illness, death of a loved one, financial trouble, or maybe a deep heartache for wayward children, God sees you. He hears your cries and will show His unfailing faithfulness to you. He holds you in his righteous right hand.

Is there something that keeps you from seeing God's unfailing faithfulness and peace? Run to Him; He will never leave you.

Prayer

Abba Father, thank You for answering my prayer and calming my fears. Strengthen those, like me, who forget You are near, even when we can't feel Your presence. Remind us there's no need to be anxious. We can bring our biggest fears or smallest problems to You with thanksgiving, knowing You will hear us and give peace. Thank You for Your unfailing faithfulness. In Jesus' name, amen.

Declare the Gospel Without Words

Heather Roberts

*"Anyone who does not love does not know God,
because God is love." 1 John 4:8 ESV*

I pulled into the driveway of the tri-level home. For the past eight weeks, I had been helping a struggling family to get it ready to sell. I didn't ring the doorbell because it only drove the dog nuts. Besides, the homeowner expected me.

"Let's tackle the laundry room today," Shirley said.

"You're in charge. What did your mom, the Realtor, say? Does she think we're getting close?" I asked.

"I don't know. Maybe after the next youth group finishes painting the downstairs, we'll better understand what else needs to be done."

Two minutes later, calf-deep in laundry, I heard a barrage of swear words and the Lord's name in vain coming from the other room. I didn't even flinch this time. I had grown accustomed to it, along with the complaints that Christians were hypocrites, living one way and condemning others for the same behavior.

"Sorry, the patch in the drywall caved in," Shirley called from the other room.

I smiled and continued to sort, content that progress was being made. Progress for the house and for my maturity as a Christ follower.

When we started the project, I never thought Shirley and I would become friends. In all of our time together, I never once brought up salvation or who Christ was, but I know she saw Christ in me and all those who helped. Not because of my might, but because of His ability to mold my heart. I know I am better because of this opportunity to love. And I am eternally grateful the Lord allowed me to learn from His example. Abba taught me to declare the gospel without words by demonstrating sacrificial love that is not easily offended.

Months earlier, my prayer time with the Lord went something like this: "But You don't understand. They take Your name in vain practically every other word. They constantly accuse Christians of leading hypocritical lives while I'm serving them."

"Daughter, have you considered I'm not offended by their behavior? You are. I am not surprised or hurt when the lost act lost. Why are you? I gave my life for those who would love and serve me and for those who would mock and kill me. Serve them anyway, as I did, with sacrificial love. The toil of your hands speaks love more than any sermon could."

The Lord had prepared me to carry out this mission with the understanding that He would teach me to love deeper than I knew how. I didn't know what that would look like, but I vaguely understood it would take more of me than I had ever given before. I would need to die to self and live for Christ.

It's easy to get offended. But in that moment, consider it a great opportunity to douse the person in grace. You don't have to deny your feelings or opinions. Keep yourself aligned to what the Scripture says about the specific situation while actively demonstrating grace and love by serving them.

The better we comprehend the love God lavishes on us, the easier it becomes to pour love out to others. He first loved us when we were incapable of showing mercy and grace because we did not comprehend it. He gathers us to Him when we are yet opposed to Him. At the cross, when they tortured and mocked Him, He prayed, "Father, forgive them; for they know not what they do" (Luke 23:34 KJV). How can we hold a lost person's actions against them when they are ignorant of God's love? The Lord patiently taught me to look past the offense and see the hurting person behind it. God loves the person who offended you more than you can fathom.

The Lord is still teaching me. And believe me, I'm listening. His loving lessons are life-altering for both me and the world. I like to think I demonstrate Christ's sacrificial love in most relationships, but when I miss the mark, I know He is faithful to grant me another lesson at His feet.

Prayer

Lord, reveal where my heart may be offended so I will forgive and release love. I want to show Your sacrificial love. In Jesus' name, amen.

Hidden Gifts from Letting Go

Dyann Shepard

"Every branch in Me that does not bear fruit He takes away; and every branch that bears fruit He prunes, that it may bear more fruit." John 15:2 NKJV

For many years I had a daily visual of God's love. It was the oak tree in our front yard. As I enjoyed my quiet time with the Lord every morning, I looked out at my tree. It was tall and strong, and it shaded our porch and home. I loved my tree. Over the years, friends began telling me the main branch, the source of the shade, was dead and needed to be removed. I couldn't let my tree go. One day, a friend came by and announced he was cutting off the dead branch. To my surprise, the tree began to thrive. It looked different, but it had a new beauty and was the beginning of many unique gifts of love, faith, trust, and provision.

Besides providing years of firewood, there has been a far more significant gift. When the branch came down, it revealed a surprise. Something I would have missed if it had remained. A beautiful heart was etched in the trunk where the tree branch had been. It was a hidden gift. Over the next twenty years, I enjoyed watching birds fly in and out of the heart as they sang their morning songs. The heart served as a sweet reminder from the Lord that when I cling too tightly to loved ones, possessions, the past, etc., I might be missing a God gift.

In John 15:2, Jesus said: "Every branch in Me that does not bear fruit He takes away; and every branch that bears fruit He prunes, that it may bear more fruit." How often have I clung to my old dead branches? I usually resist when I feel the presence of the Lord's pruning shears. I want to hold onto my old branches. I am comfortable with them. They provide emotional shade for me. However, this simple hidden treasure, this valentine on my tree, brought opportunities to share with clients and friends the gift of faith that grew from my tree. When they asked, "Did you know there is a heart on your tree?" I was able to share how the Lord stretched my faith as I began to "let go." By letting go of trying to control people and letting go of possessions precious to me, I have experienced the joy of God's provision in my life and in those I love.

My children have matured in profound ways spiritually as I have ceased holding them too tightly. And my heart tree recently helped me let go of a ministry I loved when it became apparent my husband wanted to change churches. He didn't ask me to leave, but I knew he was unhappy. I loved our church, the people, and the ministry I was involved in. I didn't want to let go. Privately, I cried and prayed. As I sat in my prayer chair looking out the window at my heart tree, I asked myself, "Am I willing to put what I've learned to the test? Am I willing to let go and have faith that God has something new for me?" After much struggle, I asked my husband to choose a new church. I told him, "As long as they love the Lord, I'll be okay."

My walk with the Lord has deepened in surprising ways. My husband was happier, more relaxed, and grew spiritually.

Many new gifts were waiting to be revealed. Missing the teaching from my former church, I felt led to reach out to friends and clients from various denominations to join me on a spiritual journey studying the Word of God. This has been enormously rewarding.

I began attending Sisters of the Heart, a women's fellowship group at our current church. This was a new experience in faith for me. After a spiritual topic is presented, each of us finds a quiet spot to meditate, pray, and journal. Later, there is a time of sharing what the Lord revealed to our hearts. This meditative, thoughtful fellowship resulted in new growth and freedom in my faith walk with the Lord. It has birthed a more profound peace and trust. I would have missed this sweet blessing of new sisters in the Lord if I had not been willing to let go of our previous church.

My tree is gone now, the victim of drought. One morning, I looked at my heart tree and realized something was terribly wrong. It had died. Once again, I cried, "No, no, not my tree." It had been a symbol of hidden gifts. Always faithfully there every morning, reminding me to be open to new things and be willing to let go of others. It couldn't be dead. But it was. Now I had to let go of the very symbol that had taught me to let go.

The morning the tree came down, my friend Ann brought me the book *The Giving Tree*. I read it through my tears. Just as the "Giving Tree" found a new purpose, my tree did as well. The Lord provided an excellent craftsman who saved the portion of the tree with the etched heart and made a beautiful bench for me.

My tree has been repurposed! My heart tree is now my heart bench. It serves as a reminder that as I walk in faith, God is faithful and has a purpose with each season of my life. I recently retired, and God has repurposed my life from CPA to writer. This might not have happened had it not been for the lessons He taught me in the hidden gifts from my oak tree.

Prayer

Father, You are the Creator of change. You give us seasons, life, and death. Let me lean on You when I'm fearful or resistant to change. I know through change, spiritual growth can happen. Lord, please help me to embrace change that brings me closer to You. In Jesus' name, amen.

How to Live in the Power of God's Lavish Love

Lyneta Smith

"May you experience the love of Christ, though it is too great to understand fully. Then you will be made complete with all the fullness of life and power that comes from God." Ephesians 3:19 NLT

In 2014, I wanted out of my story. What started as a crack in the façade of my peaceful, happy life became a torrent of formerly suppressed traumatic childhood memories. Only it didn't feel like long-ago events. In my mind, I was right back in that place, experiencing all the emotions I'd encountered as a child.

But I wasn't that child. As an adult, I had all the marks of a good Christian life. I tried to act as if I still had it all together—the homeschooling mom, the high-performing college student, the June Cleaver wife—but I could no longer deny what I'd long suspected.

All my life, I believed God merely tolerated me. He loved everyone else I knew—even thieves hanging on crosses next to the Savior. Still, I had a purpose: reforming our family legacy by bringing up my girls to love and follow Jesus. I knew He wanted my loyalty, my obedience. But I spent most of my life up to that point under the lie that I was barely cutting it.

I don't know what sparked the memories. Once they started, it seemed like a flood I couldn't hold back. Maybe it was my imminent empty nest. My youngest daughter was about to jet off to her next big adventure before college, a YWAM mission trip, leaving me with only a grumpy cat and the family dog to care for.

Meanwhile, accusing thoughts barraged me. *If people knew your dirty little secret, you'd never be accepted in church.* Or, *If your husband knew what happened to you, he'd consider you soiled—damaged goods—and then your marriage, as you know it, would be over.*

I'd worked hard to create my Christian homeschooling mom with a have-it-all-together identity. But who was I if I lost all that?

What would I be, except for that sad, abused, desperate-for-love little girl?

One day, shortly before my daughter's graduation, God spoke to me. It sounds crazy and hard to believe. I almost wouldn't believe it myself, except I was there.

I was driving home from the grocery store, praying for God to take away the pain. "Why did You make me like I am, anyway?" I asked. "Why couldn't I be like one of those ladies with her perfect childhood?"

As I pulled into the garage, God spoke to me as clear as I've ever heard any voice. "Trust me with your story," He said.

It wasn't an audible voice (thankfully—I might have fainted!) but it was so clear and unlike the negative voices barraging me that I instantly recognized it.

The voice was so close and so real that I adjusted the rearview mirror, expecting Him to be in the backseat.

It was empty. But for the first time in years, I felt God's presence.

Out of all the billions of people on the planet, He came to me. Spoke to me. "Okay, I'll trust You," I said out loud.

That was the first step in a long healing process where I gradually realized the depth of God's love. Not just for mankind in general, not just for the beautiful people who had it all together, but for the flawed, broken mess that was me. God continued to show me in many ways that He cared for my heart and loved me more than I could imagine. He couldn't love me any more or less than He already does, regardless of my doubts and questions.

Eventually, God led me to a life motivated by a love for others, which overflows from the Father. I no longer measure my worth by what I do or how people perceive me. That façade is gone.

It seems like such a basic tenet of our relationship with God: He loves us. But for many of us, our perception of His love has been warped by our experiences. Trauma, especially extended abuse, could convince us that we are undeserving of God's love.

Here's the truth: God's love does not depend on our view of ourselves. He loves us as His masterpiece that He knew inside and out before we were even born.

I believe we have an enemy who hates us so much, he would do anything to convince us God doesn't love us. The bad choices of others tend to throw the door wide open for lies and deceit. Pain from trauma can blind us to God's love. We overcome it only by the power of God.

We are made complete in Christ by that same power. No matter what happened to us in the past, we can become the person God intended by accepting and living in the deep, deep love of Christ.

Prayer

God, I know Your love for me is not diminished by past traumas, but it is reflected in Your goodness and deep affection for Your creations in Your image. May I always feel and know Your deep love that You lavish on me all of my days. Let me have eyes to see and an open heart to accept all You have to offer me. In Jesus' name, amen.

Altar-ed Conscience

Laura Smith

Therefore, if you are presenting your offering at the altar, and there you remember that your brother has something against you, leave your offering there before the altar and go; first be reconciled to your brother, and then come and present your offering." Matthew 5:23–24 NASB

As I turned into the Farmer's Choice Grocery parking lot, a truck darted directly in front of me, cutting me off. As the woman in the passenger seat glanced my way, I mustered the most horrible, displeased look possible. It was not just a scowl, but the kind where my entire face contorted in such a way there was no question as to my feelings. That will show them.

We both proceeded to park. I was hoping they would visit the gym next door. Much to my chagrin, they entered Farmer's Choice. Navigating my way through the aisles of the small store, I cringed as the couple kept appearing, aisle after aisle. Though still quite angry with them, I was also embarrassed by my behavior. However, anger was the stronger of the two. While being a tough cookie in my mind, or even in my car, angry face to prove it, I am quite wimpy in person. Hence my uncomfortable disposition each time we passed one another.

Finally, I had my groceries and headed toward the counter to check out. I was mortified to see the couple getting in line in front of me. I halted, feigning interest in whatever display was closest to me at the moment. I was rescued by another shopper who showed up just in time and got in line before me. How convenient. The display was no longer an interest to me. I found my place in line, now safe with someone between the couple and me. For the first time, a sense of relief washed over me. It was short-lived.

Suddenly in my mind, out of nowhere—"Go apologize to them." What in the world? Ummm...*no way*. Then again— "Go apologize to them."

The couple was getting ready to pay. Again, my response—*no*.

I knew the Lord, without a doubt, was speaking to me. There have been many moments I knew He was communicating with me, but it was always a feeling. A sense. An idea. But this. This was different than my other experiences. It had to be Him because I would never entertain the idea of apologizing to them. At this point, they were paying and about to make their exit. This third and final time was even clearer and firmer than the previous two.

"Go apologize to them, *now*. This is your last chance. Go." Suddenly I was a child being scolded by my loving daddy for being disobedient. There was a healthy fear. Okay.

Without hesitation, I took a deep breath, asked the person in front of me to excuse me and moseyed up to the couple as they were about to walk off. To say I was nervous would be a gross understatement. But I was even more terrified about not obeying the Lord's direct instruction.

"Excuse me. You're going to think I'm crazy, but I must apologize for the way I acted in the parking lot. I had no right to give you that hateful look. I'm sorry." I explained I was a Christian and was thoroughly embarrassed and ashamed of my behavior.

The woman was far more gracious than I had even hoped. She smiled and quickly told me it was okay, and they should not have pulled out in front of me the way they did. I accepted her apology but reiterated that my behavior was still inexcusable. We parted ways with smiles and clean consciences. I quickly made my way back to my cart.

How easy for us to act out in anger and bitterness. How difficult for us to respond with grace and forgiveness. Because we are human and live in a fallen world, we will continue to struggle with sin. We will continue to fail.

The good news is that we do not have to stay there. Though it goes against our sinful nature, our heavenly Father requires that we humble ourselves, resist our pride, and go to the person whom we have wronged. He wants our praise and worship, but only after we have dealt with our sin. We cannot control how the other person receives our admittance of wrongdoing, but the Lord is pleased with us when we humble ourselves and seek to make things right to the best of our ability. That act of faithfulness sets us back in a right relationship with Him.

Prayer

Heavenly Father, thank You for Your unfailing love and forgiveness, which we do not deserve. As we become aware of our sin against someone, give us humility so we may go to them, acknowledge our sin, and ask for their forgiveness. May we also offer forgiveness. In Jesus' name, amen.

Absence With a Purpose

Lori Ann Wood

*"He has made everything beautiful in its time. He has also
set eternity in the human heart; yet no one can fathom what
God has done from beginning to end." Ecclesiastes 3:11 NIV*

Letting go of my children exposes a raw place in my soul and
an unyielding lump in my throat. I cried every time they
started a new phase of life: preschool, kindergarten, high
school, college, and marriage. Something deep inside a parent
dies a little every time a child crosses another threshold. And
yet, deep down, we know it is how it is supposed to be. How it
must be for them to make their own decisions and their own
way in life. And we are proud to have played whatever small
part we did in their development. We are thrilled for them. We
throw parties and confetti, and we clap our hands as we wave
goodbye. But they leave a hole of what was, and I am reminded
of the strange mix that is *saudade*.

Saudade is a term that originated in Portugal. Like many
rich words, it has no English equivalent. This word came to life
in the fifteenth century when Portuguese ships sailed to Africa
and Asia, hoping to open trade routes. The family fragment

left behind shouldered a constant feeling that something big was missing from their lives, a yearning for the presence of the loved ones who had sailed. It has been called the "presence of absence."

Sending my youngest child back to Europe after Christmas break to finish her year studying abroad, I got a big dose of saudade. I wrote a note to slip into her suitcase:

In France, instead of "I miss you," people say, "You are missing from me." That's how it feels when you're not here. Part of me is missing. Something special and important. I felt it when you went to kindergarten, to college, and now again as you go back overseas. But also, it feels like part of me is on an adventure, and I love that. Stay safe, brave girl. Call me soon and tell me how our adventure is going. I love you, Mom

As parents constantly releasing little bits of our children as they grow, we understand saudade. Saudade is, at its core, about relationships. The blissful glue that binds them, and the calamity of this broken life that tears them apart. It is about missing something that cannot be replaced and feeling the gaping hole of its absence.

If you're yearning for a lost soul to return to you someday, you know saudade.

If you welcome the still-painful memories of someone who has died, you know saudade.

If you're an empty-nester waiting for future grandchildren, you know saudade.

If you endure paralyzing loneliness in the second half of a full life, you know saudade.

If you're living with chronic illness, disease, or pain, you know saudade.

If you suppress the constant feeling that something important is missing in your life, you know saudade.

If you're alive at this moment, you may not know it, but you know saudade.

That strange presence of absence will eventually affect all of our relationships. But none with more pull than our relationship with God. Wise men such as Solomon and Pascal knew about saudade.

Solomon wrote in Ecclesiastes 3:11 that God "set eternity in the human heart." Made in His image, our oneness with God was there in the beginning, but we have become separated. We were born with free will. And it had to be this way for us to truly love, to freely choose God. Until we choose Him, He and His eternal nature are missing from us. And that heart vacuum constantly aches to be filled as we yearn for an eternity we can sense, an eternity we once knew.

Modern thinkers have now acknowledged Solomon's wisdom. Psychologists confirm that human beings have a belief in eternal life hardwired into us, regardless of the amount (or complete lack of) religious exposure. We all have a longing, a knowing, for forever and the Eternal God. It just is.

We can choose to perfectly fill that hole once occupied with the Everlasting, or we can search for something else to clumsily and cheaply pour into the spot. But all the little shards of this life that we dump in will never fill that infinite vacuum.

Pascal's idea of a God-shaped vacuum in our hearts speaks to this. From his Pensees #425:

"What else does this craving, and this helplessness proclaim but that there was once in man a true happiness, of which all that now remains is the empty print and trace? This he tries in vain to fill with everything around him, seeking in things that are not there the help he cannot find in those that are, though none can help, since this infinite abyss can be filled only with an infinite and immutable object; in other words, by God himself."

Saudade is indeed absence with a presence. But it is also absence with a pull, absence for a purpose. This God-shaped space in our hearts represents the most important saudade we must deal with in this life. How we satisfy that longing will define our destiny. But we are not left in the dark as we seek to fill that void.

The most gaping hole in history was the empty tomb. Christ's tomb explains saudade. The emptiness first grieved His followers, then it saved the world. Absence with a purpose. Ironically, we all need that tomb, that hole, to understand the answer to our own heart's void. Our heart vacuum can only be filled by the One who triumphed over the ultimate emptiness. So in a real sense, it took a hole to fill a hole.

My daughter returned from Europe in one piece—more mature, more compassionate, and yes, even more independent. Just as God allows saudade in our lives for a reason, and just as the tomb was needed for the resurrection, it seems my daughter's absence had a purpose too.

Prayer

God, please guide me into a more fulfilling relationship with You. Thank You for being the answer to the deepest need of my soul. Father, please reveal to me that nothing on Earth, including my own children, can fill the hole in my heart that is meant to be filled by You alone. In Jesus' name, amen.

Contributors

Christian, Navy brat, and Navy wife **DEB GARD- NER ALLARD** traveled the USA for over twenty years with her now-retired husband, Brian, and their three children. She credits faith in God and humor for getting them through the upheavals of moving and making new friends. She enjoys reading and writing. DebGardnerAllard.com

BETTS BAKER finds life with Jesus a great adventure. She writes to encourage others to know Him better. She's published in several small print and online publications. She and her husband live in Colorado near their four children and eleven grandchildren. Her passions include Jesus, family, writing, and gardening. She currently tends a large number of jade plants.

While **LAURA L. BRADFORD** passed through deep trials, she felt the Lord nudging her to write about His divine work in her life. She laughed, thinking she lacked the skills needed, as well as the time to write. But, through Jesus' guidance, she now humbly acknowledges that hundreds of her pieces have been published.

CATHERINE ULRICH BRAKEFIELD loves Jesus. She is an award-winning author of nine books including *Wilted Dandelions, Swept into Destiny, Destiny's Whirlwind, Destiny of Heart, Waltz with Destiny,* and *Love's Final Sunrise.* Her HHH blog is the 16th of every month. She lives in Michigan with her husband, children, and grandchildren. catherineulrichbrakefield.com.

DEBRA L BUTTERFIELD is the author of ten books, which include *Claiming Her Inheritance, Discovering Her Inheritance, Unshakable Faith,* and *Carried by Grace: a Guide for Mothers of Victims of Sexual Abuse.* She is a freelance editor, the editorial director for CrossRiver Media Group and a former copywriter for Focus on the Family. DebraLButterfield.com

SANDRA KAY CHAMBERS is a wife, mother, former teacher, journalist and a nonfiction and children's author. She has published more than 700 articles and is the author of a book on prayer. Sandra is currently focusing on writing children's picture books and devotionals that help children realize they are uniquely created by God for a special purpose.

TAMARA CLYMER worked in television and newspapers, then in 2010 she founded CrossRiver Media Group, a Christian publishing company. Tami (as her friends call her) married her high school sweetheart, Shad, more than thirty years ago. She loves her husband and four kids dearly, but she also loves hot chocolate, camping, and reading. TamaraClymer.com

SALLY CRESSMAN is a multi-award-winning writer. She and her husband enjoy an easy rhythm of life as empty nesters near Nashville. You can follow her on Instagram or read about celebrating faith, family, and home. SallyCressman.com

LAUREN CREWS is passionate about God's word and teaching the Jewish roots of the Christian faith. As a women's ministry leader, speaker, Bible teacher, and public-school teacher Lauren is equipped to share deep Christian truths. Lauren lives in Florida with her husband and two brown dogs, who have their humans well trained. LaurenCrews.com

TRACY CRUMP dispenses hope in her multi-award-winning book, *Health, Healing, and Wholeness: Devotions of Hope in the Midst of Illness.* She's published more than thirty anthology stories. Tracy proofreads and edits for clients, and blogs for caregivers, but her most important job is grandma to five completely unspoiled grandchildren. TracyCrump.com

SHARON DAVIS grew up in South Georgia when Sunday afternoons were spent visiting neighbors on the front porch. A retired pharmacist, she divides her time between writing, grandchildren, and church. She has devotions published in christiandevotions.us and a short story in *When Life Gives You Lemons: Short Stories to Make You Smile.* SharonDavisWriter.com

DEEDEE LAKE

DAWN MARIE DAY is a professor of nursing and the Chair of graduate nursing programs at a small Christian university. She lives in North Carolina with her husband, loves her two children and their incredible spouses. Her three grandsons completely own her heart! She enjoys writing, reading, camping, hiking, playing murder mystery games, and giving God glory.

As a former educator and librarian, **JARM DEL BOCCIO** gives young readers a fresh perspective of history, offering them a real-life hero in her award-winning middle grade novel, *The Heart Changer.* Now, in her silver years, she looks forward—not backward. With transparency and passion, Jarem helps maturing women flourish in God's glory. JarmDelBoccio.com

BECKY HITCHCOCK, a retired judicial secretary, lives and writes in Georgia. She and her high school sweetheart husband, Keith, have two grown daughters. Whether penning articles or fiction, Becky feels God smiling when she writes. She still takes time to sip tea, walk a beach, and search for vintage Blue Willow china. SensitiveonPurpose.blogspot.com

LOLLIE HOFER and her husband, Mike, live in Nebraska and have two adult children and four grandchildren. She has been published in several well-known devotional sites. Three devotions are published in a book through Wholly Loved Ministries entitled, *Drawing Near: 90 Day Devotional.* Lollie writes articles too. LollieHoferAuthor.com

ABBA'S LESSONS

PENNY L. HUNT is an award-winning, best-selling author, speaker, blogger, and a grateful grandma. She enjoys writing with the hope of bringing glory to God and encouragement. Penny lives between a railroad track and a peach orchard in rural South Carolina with her husband, Bill, a retired career naval officer and attaché, and their two dogs. PennyLHunt.com

MARY-ANNE RUBADO KLINE, a Florida native, now Colorado transplant, is married to her kinsman redeemer, Jeremiah. They have four beautiful children: Ethan, Andrea, Jensen, and Maggie. She's a stay-at-home mom, military and first responder's wife, and Iraqi war widow. Mary-Anne enjoys serving in church, hiking, and of course, the Rocky Mountains.

RITA KLUNDT became an author, speaker, and story collector after thirty years of nursing. Her memoir, *Goliath's Mountain,* is a view into the life of a woman touched by mental illness and suicide. Rita and her husband live in central Illinois. They enjoy travel and are excited about where this stage of life and story collecting is taking them. RitaKlundt.com

Queen of Fun and Coffee Cup Philosopher, **CATHY KRAFVE** understands authentic conversation and communication are your way to a delightful marriage. She hosts Fireside Talk Radio, a weekly blog and podcast. With her knack for laughter and storytelling, Cathy puts a snappy spin on deeply spiritual truths. Truth with a Texas twang!

137

DEEDEE LAKE is a storyteller, speaker, author, blogger, columnist, Christian life coach who has been married forty years. She also speaks and writes about relationships as the author of the *Rules of Engagement* series. A navy brat, DeeDee jumped ship and married her Army pilot. She's lived in more than fifty houses and still loves to move her furniture. DeeDeeLake.com

ESTHER LOVEJOY is a frequent retreat and conference speaker with over thirty years of ministry experience. Her passion is to encourage women in their journey with God through her speaking and writing. She is the author of three books including *Big Steps, Little Steps* and *An Unnatural Beauty*. Esther shares her journey with God on viewfromthesparrowsnest.com

CAROL OGLE MCCRACKEN is a speaker, Bible teacher, and author who brings to life the written Word of God. Her authentic challenges faced while journeying through alcoholism, raising a special-needs child, and divorce, equipped her to teach, entertain and encourage you. Carol's passion is to make the Bible come alive for women.

ALICE H. MURRAY is an adoption attorney who is also passionate about writing. She wrote for Adoption.com, blogs AliceinWonderingland.Wordpress.com, and pieces published in several books, magazines, and online. Alice is an officer and board member of the Florida Adoption Council and of Hope Global Initiative.

CHERYL PADEN is a fourth generation Nebraskan with a special love for the state's history, antiques, and the simple life Nebraska offers. Cheryl writes inspirational, devotional, and memoir. She has published her work in magazines, anthologies, and devotional books. Cheryl has worked as a registered nurse, in apartment management, bookkeeping, and pastor.

After thirty-eight years of marriage, six children, and nine grandchildren **NORMA POORE** is still crazy about her knight in shining armor, David. Her favorite thing to do is to cook for and hang out with her large family. NormaPoore.com

HEATHER ROBERTS is the mother of four and the wife to an amazing husband. She loves to read and garden and is always scoping out other people's landscapes. Chocolate is her arch-nemesis, and she cherishes time spent in the pursuit of God's voice. She writes about the encouraging insights the Lord has graciously given her. HeatherNRoberts.com

DYANN SHEPARD is a wife, mother, grandmother, writer, speaker, Bible teacher, former Stephen's Minister, and retired CPA. Her passion is writing about experiencing God's presence in our daily lives as we open our hearts to Him. She's the author of *Wisdom: Capturing the Power of our Words*. She writes a monthly blog at PersonalParables.com

LYNETA SMITH is the author of multiple award-winning books including *Curtain Call: A Memoir*. Lyneta and husband, Doug, are happy empty nesters living in middle Tennessee. As a writer and editor, she loves the flexibility to enjoy the grandma life. Look for her at the coffee shop with friends or teaching Bible study.

As a Christ follower, **LAURA SMITH**'s adult life has been spent teaching in some capacity. She and her husband, Joel, have two wonderful adult children and enjoy the empty nest phase of life. Her hobbies include reading Christian novels, journaling, watching movies, '70s TV shows, eating out, and kayaking in North Carolina.

An award-winning writer and mom to three great young adults, **LORI ANN WOOD** lives in Arkansas with her husband. She serves with two heart associations, and is the author of *Divine Detour: The path you'd never choose can lead to the faith you've always wanted*. Lori Ann writes to encourage deep faith questions along the detours of life. LoriAnnWood.com

Answers, gifts, lessons love and promises...

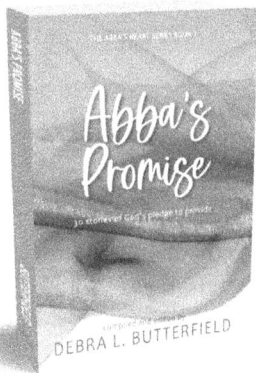

Abba's Answers
DEBRA L. BUTTERFIELD

Abba's Gifts
TAMARA CLYMER

Abba's Heart
TAMARA CLYMER

Abba's Lessons
DEE DEE LAKE

Abba's Promise
DEBRA L. BUTTERFIELD

Abba's Devotion series

Available in bookstores and online retailers.

"soul-searching"

"vulnerable"

UNCOVER YOUR DIVINE DESIGN

Who did God create you to be?

"highly recommend it!"

Available in bookstores and from online retailers.

CR CrossRiver Media
www.crossrivermedia.com

Discover more great books at
CrossRiverMedia.com

RADIANT INFLUENCE

If you feel like your life is boring and God would never use you, you have a lot in common with a girl named Esther. Her story is one of courage, faith, and identity. It's a tale of the incredible hand of an invisible God working in the lives of those who trust Him. As she stepped out in faith, Esther discovered who God had made her, a woman of influence. Do you want your life to be filled with purpose? If so, come journey through this study of Esther and discover that you have more in common with this beauty queen than you think.

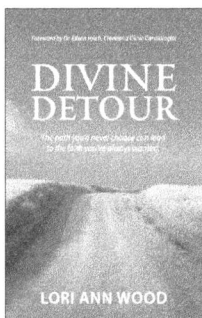

DIVINE DETOUR

Why trust a God who disappoints? A serious medical diagnosis took Lori Ann Wood on a faith detour she never saw coming. As a lifelong believer, she felt profound disappointment in the God she thought she knew. *Divine Detour* is the result of Lori Ann's risky decision to embrace difficult questions. Come along on a forty-day journey deep into the heart of a God who often doesn't behave as we'd like. You'll learn to embrace the three questions every life encounters so your faith can thrive along your own inevitable detour.

BIG STEPS LITTLE STEPS

Discover *Big Steps, Little Steps,* a topical devotional that allows you to turn to any page you like on any day you like. We're often jostled by the demands and worries of life. Think of this as a guilt-free devotional. The pages aren't dated, so you'll never be behind. These 12-weeks of devotions cover a broad range of topics we all encounter on our journey with God. God has promised to guide us, whether our steps are big or little. Both lead us forward. Both lead to Him. Not every step is easy, but every step is worth it!

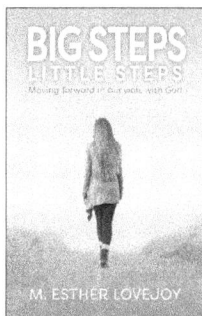

www.ingramcontent.com/pod-product-compliance
Lightning Source LLC
Chambersburg PA
CBHW061828040426
42447CB00012B/2865

9 7 8 1 9 3 6 5 0 1 8 7 8